THE BASICS AND BEYOND

PRACTICAL WRITING ACTIVITIES
FOR TODAY AND TOMORROW

OTHER GOODYEAR BOOKS IN LANGUAGE ARTS & READING

DO YOU READ ME?   Practical Approaches to Teaching Reading Comprehension
Arnold A. Griese

I CAN MAKE IT ON MY OWN   Functional Reading Ideas and Activites for Daily Survival
Michelle Berman and Linda Shevitz

GALAXY OF GAMES   For Reinforcing Writing Skills
Jerry Mallett

IMAGINE THAT!   Illustrated Poems and Creative Learning Experiences
Joyce King and Carol Katzman

LANGUAGE ARTS IDEA BOOK   Classroom Activities for Children
Joanne Schaff

MAINSTREAMING LANGUAGE ARTS AND SOCIAL STUDIES   Special Ideas and Activities for the Whole Class
Anne H. Adams, Charles R. Coble, Paul B. Hounshell

MAKING KIDS CLICK   Independent Activities in Reading and the Language Arts
Linda Polon and Aileen Cantwell

NEW DIMENSIONS IN ENGLISH   An Ideabook of Language Arts Activities for Middle and Secondary School Teachers
Joanne Schaff

OUNCE OF PREVENTION PLUS A POUND OF CURE   Tests and Techniques for Aiding Individual Readers
Ronald W. Bruton

PHORGAN'S PHONICS
Harry W. Forgan

READING CORNER   Ideas, Games, and Activities for Individualizing Reading
Harry W. Forgan

SUCCESS IN READING AND WRITING SERIES
Anne H. Adams, Elizabeth Bebensee, Helen Cappleman, Judith Connors, Mary Johnson

READING FOR SURVIVAL IN TODAY'S SOCIETY   Volumes I and II
Anne H. Adams, Anne Flowers, Elsa E. Woods

TOTALACTION   Ideas and Activities for Teaching Children Ages Five to Eight
Pat Short and Billee Davidson

WRITE UP A STORM   Creative Writing Ideas and Activities for the Middle Grades
Linda Polon and Aileen Cantwell

WRITING CORNER
Arnold Cheyney

For information about these or other Goodyear books in Science, Math, Social Studies, General Methods, and Centers, write to

> Janet Jackson
> Goodyear Publishing Company
> 1640 Fifth Street
> Santa Monica, CA 90401

THE BASICS AND BEYOND

Practical Writing Activities for Today and Tomorrow

Linda Shevitz
Michelle Berman

Illustrated by
David Carmen Longo

GOODYEAR PUBLISHING COMPANY, INC.
SANTA MONICA, CALIFORNIA 90401

To our children,
Beth,
Julie,
and Greg
with the hope
that they will
enrich their life experiences
as they move
from the "basics" to "beyond."

Words are the bridges we build
To reach each other.
            from "The Written Word"
            by Mary O'Neill

Never let a thought shrivel and die
For want of a way to say it,
For English is a wonderful game
And all of you can play it.
            from "The Wonderful Words"
            by Mary O'Neill

Library of Congress Cataloging in Publication Data

Shevitz, Linda.
    The basics and beyond.

    1. English language—Composition and exercises.
    I. Berman, Michelle, joint author.   II. Title.
PE1413.S52   808'.042   80-28684
ISBN O-8302-0992-1

Copyright © 1981 by Goodyear Publishing Company, Inc.
Santa Monica, California 90401

ISBN: 0-8302-0992-1
Y-0992-1
Current printing (last digit):
10 9 8 7 6 5 4 3 2 1
Printed in the United States of America
Introductory quotations from Mary O'Neill, *Words, Words, Words,* © 1966, Doubleday and Co., New York.
"The Spirit of Aloha" from William Knowlton, *Hawaii: Pacific Wonderland,* © 1962, Dodd, Mead & Co., New York.
Telegram forms courtesy of Western Union.
Change of Address Kit forms courtesy of the U.S. Post Office, Greenbelt, Maryland.

Contents

Introduction for Teachers

PURPOSE

In order to function most effectively in today's complex society, students need to develop a variety of writing skills to use in their daily lives. *The Basics and Beyond* presents motivational real-world activities to help upper elementary and junior high school students build these needed practical written expression skills. The book, containing reproducible student worksheets, is intended as a supplemental resource tool for reinforcing and enriching a regular classroom language arts program, rather than as a textbook for introducing specific writing skills.

ORGANIZATION

The activities in *The Basics and Beyond* are organized into two major units, each with a particular emphasis. In Unit 1 students build basic skills in grammar and usage, and gain experience in sentence construction. In Unit 2 students go *beyond* acquiring a knowledge of *basic* writing skills to actually applying those skills to situations encountered in their daily lives. Each unit is further divided into sections, each of which stresses specific writing skills.

Unit 1—Today: Develop Your Skills
Section One
Traveling Through the World of Words
All activities in this section are related to the real-world theme of a trip to Hawaii, in which the eight *parts of speech* and *special types of words* (synonyms, antonyms, homophones, words with affixes) are presented.
Section Two
Communicating Through the World of Sentences
All activities in this section are related to communication media such as newspapers, magazines, television, and movies. Exercises present *sentence foundations* (subjects, predicates, phrases, clauses), *sentence structures* (simple, compound, complex), *sentence functions* (statement, command, question, exclamation), and *sentence features* (capitalization, punctuation).

Unit 2—Tomorrow: Apply Your Skills
Section One
The Real World: Recording Personal Information
Activities in this section include writing schedules, calendars, logs, journals, lists, and resumés.

Section Two
The Real World: Responding to the Demands of Society
Activities in this section include five areas:
1. Writing Messages—telephone messages, memos, notices, announcements
2. Writing Correspondence—invitations, greeting cards, notes, postcards, telegrams, personal and business letters
3. Writing Directions—product directions, task directions, skill directions, place location directions
4. Outlining
5. Completing Forms—request forms, personal information and consumer forms, applications, opinion polls, order forms, financial forms

FORMAT

Each activity or set of activities is reproducible and includes the following:
1. Definitions of terms   ‖ double boxed ‖

2. Examples   │ single boxed │

3. Directions (marked by a star ★ in the margin)

4. Answer Key (found in the back of the book)

While many activities are self-checking, several are open-ended (particularly those in Unit 2) and have no single "right" answers. These activities are marked ☑ in the Answer Keys, directing students to check their answers with a teacher. Several activities also include specially marked

__BONUS__ exercises, which provide additional enrichment and challenge, and promote critical and creative thinking. At the end of the book are two appendices. Appendix A is a proofreading guide for students to use in evaluating their own written work, and Appendix B presents some additional ideas and resources for teachers in developing practical writing programs.

SKILL DEVELOPMENT

The Basics and Beyond presents activities to help students develop a variety of competencies in the area of practical written expression. The first unit builds basic skills of grammar and sentence structure, while the second unit goes *beyond the basics* of skill-building to real-world application of skills.

The major competencies developed in *The Basics and Beyond* are listed below.

Unit 1
Section One
- Identifying and correctly using the eight parts of speech
- Identifying and correctly using synonyms, antonyms, homophones, compound words, and affixes

Section Two
- Identifying and writing simple subjects and predicates, complete subjects and predicates, phrases, dependent clauses, and independent clauses
- Completing and constructing simple, compound, and complex sentences
- Completing and constructing declarative (statement), interrogative (question), imperative (command), and exclamatory (exclamation) sentences
- Correctly using capital letters
- Correctly using punctuation marks, including the period, question mark, exclamation point, comma, quotation marks, apostrophe, semicolon, colon, dash, ellipsis, and parentheses

Unit 2
Section One
- Completing personal schedules and calendars
- Writing log and journal entries
- Organizing information through categorizing and listing
- Completing personal resumes

Section Two
- Writing messages for others, including memos, telephone messages, notices, announcements, and posters
- Writing correspondence, including invitations, notes (of response, thanks, and congratulations), greeting cards, postcards, telegrams, personal letters, business letters (of request, response and criticism)
- Writing directions, including how to use products, complete tasks, master skills, and move from one location to another
- Writing and using outlines, including constructing outlines from written material and writing paragraphs based on outlines
- Correctly completing forms, including request forms, personal information forms, consumer forms, applications, opinion polls, order forms, and financial forms (sales reports, bills, checks, and deposit slips)

UTILIZATION OF MATERIALS

The reproducible materials in *The Basics and Beyond* are suitable for large groups, small groups, or independent use. The activities may be presented directly from the book, at learning centers, or as handouts for independent work. While activities are basically self-directed, some students may need assistance in interpreting definitions and directions. Based on your assessment of students' individual skill levels, you may also find it necessary to provide additional instruction prior to students' completion of some activities. While aimed primarily at upper elementary and junior high school students, activities may also be appropriate for some high school and adult education classes.

Unit 1
Section One
These basic grammar and usage activities related to a trip to Hawaii are suitable for presentation as single exercises or as part of a continuous sequential skill program. Since the sequential development would be based on the skill level of the students, you could initiate activities at any suitable point in this section. It should be noted that since definitions of terms are given only once, it may be necessary to refer students back to

previously stated definitions. While students may not be familiar with many Hawaiian names used in this section, field-testing of these activities indicated that vocabulary familiarity did not affect students' success or enjoyment in completing the exercises. This particularly applied to the motivational game, "Hawaiian Island Hop," which is presented as a culminating activity for learning parts of speech.

Section Two
Although the activities in this section can be presented as single exercises, the parts on sentence foundations (subject, predicates, clauses) and sentence structures (simple, compound, and complex sentences) may be more effective if presented in sequence. The parts on sentence functions (statements, questions, commands, exclamations) and sentence features (capitalization and punctuation) are more readily adaptable as single activities. As in Section One, some activities serve as a review of previously presented skills, and students may have to refer back to definitions of terms listed in earlier activities.

Unit 2
In this unit, students may be given choices of activities based on their abilities, interests, and needs. These materials should be utilized in whatever ways seem most meaningful to you.

Appendix A—Practical Proofreading
You may wish to reproduce this page for students to use with activities throughout the book. Consistent use of the guide is intended to help build proofreading skills while increasing the accuracy of the student's work.

Appendix B—Additional Practical Writing Ideas and Resources
This list is a reference for you to use in developing and expanding your own programs for building written expression skills.

CONCLUSION
By helping build student competencies in several practical areas of written expression, *The Basics and Beyond* aims to increase individuals' confidence and independence in responding to everyday real-world situations. We hope that the activities in the book will interest and challenge your students. We have thoroughly enjoyed developing these materials, and we invite you and your students to use the exercises to go "Beyond the Basics" in finding both satisfaction and enjoyment in daily writing experiences.

Introduction for *Students*

WHAT IS THE PURPOSE OF THE BOOK?
The Basics and Beyond is a book of special writing activities concerned with experiences that you might have in your day-to-day life. Every time you fill out a form, make a list, complete a schedule, write an invitation, or compose a letter you are using *practical writing skills* to help you communicate your thoughts and ideas. To live a better life in our world you not only need to learn several *basic* writing skills, but you also need to go *beyond* knowing these basics to using or applying them. The purpose of *The Basics and Beyond* is to help you *develop* your practical writing skills, then to *apply* them. This will help you gain independence and confidence in dealing with the real world.

HOW IS THE BOOK ORGANIZED?
The book is divided into two main units, each with a special purpose. The first unit is related to developing writing skills, and the second to applying writing skills. The units are also divided into sections, each stressing a particular skill.

Unit 1—Today: Develop Your Skills
Section One
Traveling Through the World of Words
Take an imaginary trip to Hawaii as you learn about *parts of speech* (such as nouns and verbs) and about *special words* (such as synonyms and antonyms).

Section Two
Communicating Through the World of Sentences
Become a *sentence* expert as you explore newspapers, television, magazines, newspapers, and advertisements. *Capitalize* on your experience as you learn where to place *punctuation* and capital letters.

Unit 2—Tomorrow: Apply Your Skills
Organize your life as you learn how to write *schedules, calendars, journals, logs,* and *lists.* Express yourself by writing *messages, notices, invitations, postcards, greeting cards, telegrams,* and *letters.* Take charge as you improve your ability to write *directions,* make *outlines,* and fill out a variety of *forms.*

HOW ARE THE ACTIVITIES ORGANIZED?
Each activity (or set of activities) includes the following items to help you complete and check that activity.

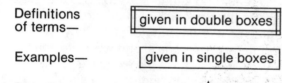

Definitions of terms— | given in double boxes

Examples— | given in single boxes

Directions—marked by a star ★ in the margin of each page

Answer Key—found in the back of the book

HOW ARE THE ACTIVITIES COMPLETED?
You will explore a *variety of ways* to complete exercises, such as filling in blanks, matching items, completing statements, doing puzzles, designing products, expressing opinions, writing jokes, playing games, making outlines, and filling out forms. Some activities have items marked **BONUS**, which give you special opportunities to use your creativity and imagination.

If you are not sure of the meaning of some of the words used in an activity, you might need to refer to definitions given in an earlier activity, or to check meanings with a dictionary or a teacher. You may also want to use the *proofreading guide* provided at the back of the book to help you review and edit your own written work.

HOW ARE THE ANSWER KEYS USED?

Answer Keys are provided for you to use in checking activities on your own. However, several exercises (particularly those in Unit 2) ask you to write your own statements, ideas, or opinions, and have no single "right" answer. These items are marked ✐ in the Answer Keys, and should be checked with a teacher.

CONCLUSION

We hope that you will enjoy completing the activities in *The Basics and Beyond,* and we think that you'll be surprised to discover how many ways writing is used in your daily life. Now we invite you to go *beyond the basics* of learning writing skills as you become involved with writing for your own satisfaction and enjoyment!

Acknowledgments

We gratefully acknowledge the assistance of the following persons:

The dedicated educators who helped us develop and evaluate our materials—Luna Coleman, Janet Johnson, Jo Campa, Sharon Upton, and Betty Morton.

The creative students who field-tested our activities—Julie, Greg, Beth, Jeff, Kim, Keith, Kenny, Darryl, Susan, Karen, Jenny, Rhonda, Carole, Christine, Buffy, Wade, Noreen, Susan, Larry, Amy, Stacy, Lisa, Debbie, Laurie, Michael, Tommy, Betsy, Kristin, Jay, Eric, Matthew, Mitu, Carl, Orna, Mark, Tanya, Keith, Teddy, Gerard, Rusty, Cheryl, Melissa, Nicki, Paul, Donald, Joel, Melissa, Marla, Brent, Kiran, Chester, Carey, Brian, Ronit, Gina, Tom, Chip, Ari, Francie, Alice, Danny, Chuck, and Topher.

Our fine typist, Karen Balamaci.

Our families, whose patience and encouragement were invaluable.

We offer a special thanks to **our gifted and talented illustrator,** Dave Longo, whose creative ability brings written words to life and beyond.

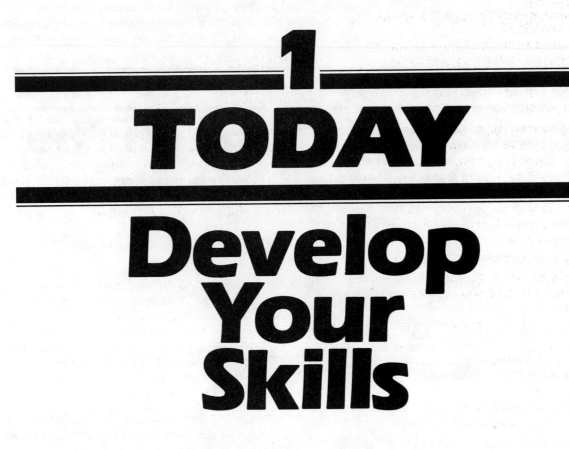

1 TODAY

Develop Your Skills

S E C T I O N   O N E
Traveling Through the World of Words

Vacation with Nouns

A **NOUN** is a word that names a person, place, or thing. A **COMMON NOUN** is any person, place, or thing, while a **PROPER NOUN** tells the name of a specific person, place, or thing. A **PROPER NOUN** begins with a capital letter.

EXAMPLES:	COMMON NOUNS	PROPER NOUNS	
	country	United States	
	state	Hawaii	
	tourists	Beth, Greg	
	volcano	Mauna Loa	

LEARN MORE ABOUT HAWAII AS YOU BEGIN YOUR HAWAIIAN HOLIDAY!

★ **PART I:** Read the travel brochure below describing the Hawaiian Islands. Find all of the nouns in each sentence and list them under the proper heading (Common Nouns or Proper Nouns). Note that the answer blanks for each sentence indicate the correct number of proper and common nouns found in that sentence.

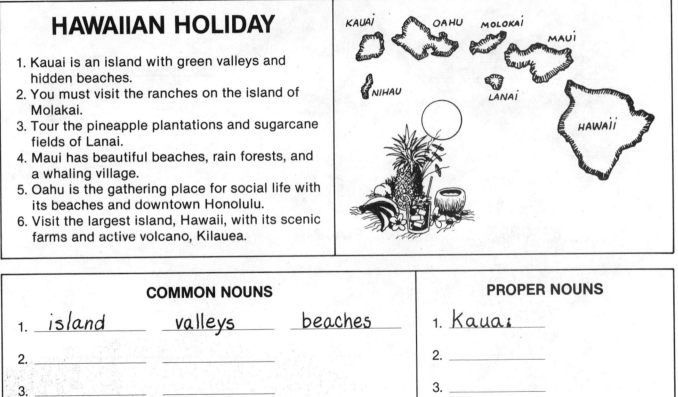

HAWAIIAN HOLIDAY

1. Kauai is an island with green valleys and hidden beaches.
2. You must visit the ranches on the island of Molakai.
3. Tour the pineapple plantations and sugarcane fields of Lanai.
4. Maui has beautiful beaches, rain forests, and a whaling village.
5. Oahu is the gathering place for social life with its beaches and downtown Honolulu.
6. Visit the largest island, Hawaii, with its scenic farms and active volcano, Kilauea.

COMMON NOUNS	**PROPER NOUNS**
1. island valleys beaches	1. Kauai
2.	2.
3.	3.
4.	4.
5.	5.
6.	6.

From *The Basics and Beyond* © 1981, Goodyear Publishing Co., Inc.

★ **PART II:** Read the paragraph below from a book about Hawaii. Underline all of the nouns in the paragraph. Select and list three of the underlined nouns under each proper heading of Persons, Places, and Things.

The Spirit of Aloha

The Hawaiian Islands tower green and high above a lonely stretch of the earth's vastest ocean. From their fringing reefs of coral to the crests of their mighty mountains, the islands are many things to many people. To earth scientists, they are a living laboratory where grow thousands of plants and animals found nowhere else in the world. To Mark Twain, Hawaii was ". . . the loveliest fleet of islands that lie anchored in any ocean." To many Americans, Hawaii, the fiftieth state in the Union, is home.

From *Hawaii: Pacific Wonderland* by William Knowlton

PERSONS

_____
_____
_____

PLACES

_____
_____
_____

THINGS

_____
_____
_____

Pronoun Holiday

A **PRONOUN** is a word that is used in place of a noun.

EXAMPLES: The family (noun) took a long vacation (noun).
They (pronoun) thoroughly enjoyed it (pronoun).

Some common **PRONOUNS** are:

I	me	my	mine	we	us	our	ours
you	your	yours	he	she	it	him	
her	his	hers	its	they	them		
this	those	these	that	theirs			

JOIN ALOHA TOURS ON A HAWAIIAN HOLIDAY!

★ **PART I:** Read the Aloha Tours announcement below. Choose pronouns from the list above to fill in the blanks in the following paragraph. Note that some of the pronouns will be used more than once.

From *The Basics and Beyond* © 1981, Goodyear Publishing Co., Inc.

When you visit Hawaii on an Aloha Tours Hawaiian Holiday, _____ will see the islands as _____
                                                              1   2

have never been seen before! Relax, and let Aloha Tours whisk _____ away on a magic carpet, as
                                                                3

_____ show _____ a tropical paradise in all of _____ splendor. _____ guarantee that
       4   5   6   7

_____ will say, " _____ always dreamed of a vacation like _____." Each tour host and hostess
       8   9   10

will do _____ or _____ best to provide for _____ every convenience. _____ enjoyment
           11   12   13   14

is _____ goal here at Aloha Tours. _____ promise that a most exotic adventure awaits _____.
       15   16   17

To enjoy _____ vacation to the fullest, just count on _____!
             18   19

" WE MAKE IT EASY FOR YOU ! "

★ **PART II:** Read the paragraph below describing one activity offered by Aloha Tours. Edit the paragraph to make it sound better by replacing each underlined noun or group of words with a pronoun. You may use the list of "common pronouns" to help you.

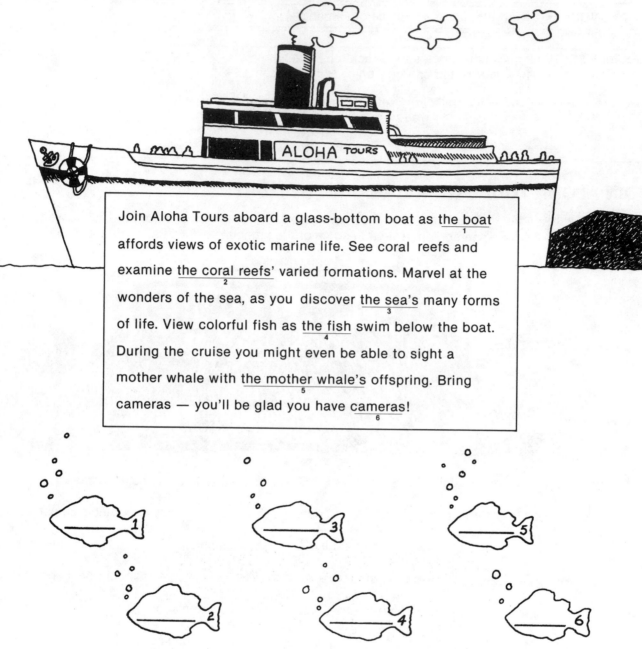

Join Aloha Tours aboard a glass-bottom boat as the boat
                                                    1
affords views of exotic marine life. See coral reefs and
examine the coral reefs' varied formations. Marvel at the
              2
wonders of the sea, as you discover the sea's many forms
                                              3
of life. View colorful fish as the fish swim below the boat.
                                    4
During the cruise you might even be able to sight a
mother whale with the mother whale's offspring. Bring
                          5
cameras — you'll be glad you have cameras!
                                          6

From *The Basics and Beyond* © 1981, Goodyear Publishing Co., Inc.

Highlighting Hawaii with Verbs

A **VERB** is a word that shows action or a state of being.

EXAMPLES:	ACTION	BEING VERBS
	swim	is
	climb	are
	enjoy	was
	cruise	has been

READ AN AIRLINES TRAVEL BROCHURE TO FIND OUT WHAT THE ISLAND OF OAHU IS REALLY LIKE!

★ **PART I:** List action verbs that you might use related to the activities pictured on the "Highlighting Hawaii" map of Oahu, one of the Hawaiian Islands. Write an action verb next to each numbered space that corresponds to a numbered illustration.

Note: Use only one word for each answer, and do not use words that end in "ing."

Example: ① 🎥 1. _snap_____ (or "click," "pose," "view," etc.)

1. _____   4. _____   7. _____   10. _____

2. _____   5. _____   8. _____   11. _____

3. _____   6. _____   9. _____   12. _____

★ **PART II:** After reading the information from the "Highlighting Hawaii" travel brochure, list all of the verbs that you find. Remember that each sentence must contain at least one verb.

HIGHLIGHTING HAWAII

Come and fly to the beautiful island of Oahu in the state of Hawaii, and enjoy some of the many delightful activities. Although it is only the third largest island, over three-quarters of Hawaii's population lives on this highly popular island. There are many wonderful experiences here for your enjoyment.

As you approach the island from the air, you will see Diamond Head, our dormant volcano, as it stands majestically etched along the coast. Waikiki Beach is our entertainment, hotel, and shopping center. Shop leisurely in the many picturesque settings.

Pearl Harbor has been a landmark on our island for many years. Tour the famous harbor and hear the story of the war activities that happened on that doomed day in 1941. Rent a car, drive around, and visit the pineapple plantations. Taste the delicious pineapple juice which is famous throughout the world. While in your car, search for scenic coves and lagoons that are hidden throughout the island.

See the fascinating highlights of Hawaii, and your vacation will be an unforgettable experience!

From The Basics and Beyond © 1981, Goodyear Publishing Co., Inc.

VERBS

1. _come_
2. _____
3. _____
4. _____
5. _____
6. _____
7. _____
8. _____
9. _____
10. _____
11. _____
12. _____

13. _____
14. _____
15. _____
16. _____
17. _____
18. _____
19. _____
20. _____
21. _____
22. _____
23. _____
24. _____
25. _____

8   UNIT 1/SECTION 1/Traveling Through the World of Words

Cook with Grammar
(Nouns and Verbs Review)

HAWAIIAN SUPPER SUPREME

Ingredients

2 lbs. chicken parts

2 tbs. butter

1 medium green pepper, cut in strips

1 can (13½ oz.) pineapple chunks

4 tsp. vinegar

2 tbs. cornstarch

2 tbs. brown sugar

½ tsp. salt

2 tsp. mustard

Directions

Melt butter in skillet. Saute chicken until browned, then stir in green pepper. Meanwhile drain pineapple. Measure pineapple syrup and add water to syrup to make 1⅓ cups. Blend syrup mixture, vinegar, cornstarch, brown sugar, salt, and mustard. Pour over chicken. Cook and stir until sauce is thickened. Cover and simmer 10 minutes. Then add pineapple. Serve over hot cooked rice.

PREPARE A HAWAIIAN MEAL AND COOK WITH GRAMMAR!

★ **PART I:** Read the directions for making "Hawaiian Supper Supreme." Find the words that tell you what things you will use in preparing the dinner (nouns), then locate the words that tell you what actions (verbs) to do while following the recipe. Place all of the listed recipe words below under the proper headings.

melt	butter	skillet	saute	chicken	stir	pepper	drain	pineapple	measure
syrup	add	water	cups	blend	mixture	vinegar	cornstarch	sugar
mustard	pour	cook	stir	sauce	cover	simmer	minutes	serve	rice

NOUNS	VERBS

From *The Basics and Beyond* © 1981, Goodyear Publishing Co., Inc.

★ **PART II:** Match the nouns with the verbs used in the recipe for Hawaiian Supper Supreme by placing the correct letter next to each numbered item.

	NOUNS		VERBS
___ 1.	butter	a.	saute
___ 2.	chicken	b.	add
___ 3.	syrup mixture	c.	drain
___ 4.	pineapple	d.	stir
___ 5.	sauce	e.	melt
___ 6.	water	f.	blend

BONUS

★ **PART III:** Create your own Hawaiian recipe using pineapple, which is a popular fruit on the Hawaiian Islands. Some suggested recipes are "Aloha Sundae," "Tropical Fruit Salad," or "Pineapple Milk Shake." After listing the recipe ingredients and writing the directions, list (under separate headings) all nouns and verbs used in your recipe.

Here's what's cookin'_____

Recipe from:_____ Serves:____

_____
_____
_____
_____
_____
_____
_____
_____
_____

NOUNS	VERBS

From *The Basics and Beyond* © 1981, Goodyear Publishing Co., Inc.

Aloha Adventures with Adjectives and Adverbs

> An **ADJECTIVE** is a word which describes, or modifies, a noun or pronoun. **ADJECTIVES** tell "what kind," "how many," or "which one."

EXAMPLES:	WHAT KIND	HOW MANY	WHICH ONE
	terrific	few	that
	colorful	several	this
	exciting	fifteen	those

ALOHA-TOURS
INFORMATION BOARD
WATER ACTIVITIES

Try these exciting water activities! Dive and swim anywhere in refreshing clear blue waters, or leisurely snorkel in many of the hidden beach coves. For a real adventure, smoothly sail on a catamaran under the tropical sun. Surf on a small tame crest of water, or watch the expert surfers as they bravely ride on the swiftly challenging crests of the white breakers around the islands. Slowly cruise on a glass-bottom boat and casually view the many unusual tropical fish found here in Hawaii. If you dare, scuba dive and carefully encounter rare fish seldom seen by visitors. Observe curious and interesting underwater coral formations and the exotically colored marine life. Finally, try your luck at the spectacular ocean fishing!

ENJOY YOURSELF! DISCOVER SOME ADVENTURES THAT AWAIT YOU IN HAWAII

★ **PART I:** Read the Water Activities material posted on the Aloha Tours Information Board. Match the listed adjectives with the nouns that they modify in the Water Activities paragraph. Place the correct letter next to each numbered noun. (Note: Some nouns may be matched with more than one adjective.)

NOUNS

____ 1. activities
____ 2. waters
____ 3. coves
____ 4. adventure
____ 5. surfers
____ 6. crests
____ 7. breakers
____ 8. fish
____ 9. formations
____ 10. life

ADJECTIVES

a. expert
b. real
c. many
d. hidden
e. tropical
f. exciting
g. underwater
h. unusual
i. challenging
j. white
k. marine
l. blue

An **ADVERB** is a word that describes, or modifies, a verb, an adjective, or another adverb. **ADVERBS** tell "how," "how much," "where," and "when."

EXAMPLES:	HOW	HOW MUCH	WHERE	WHEN
	slowly	often	there	yesterday
	quickly	frequently	here	soon
	smoothly	seldom	anywhere	later

★ **PART II:** Using the Water Activities material posted on the Aloha Tours Information Board, match the listed adverbs with the verbs or adjectives that they modify in the Water Activities paragraph. Place the correct letter next to each numbered adverb.

ADVERBS	VERBS AND ADJECTIVES
___ 1. anywhere	a. colored
___ 2. leisurely	b. encounter
___ 3. smoothly	c. ride
___ 4. bravely	d. cruise
___ 5. swiftly	e. dive, swim
___ 6. slowly	f. challenging
___ 7. casually	g. try
___ 8. here	h. sail
___ 9. carefully	i. snorkel
___ 10. seldom	j. view
___ 11. exotically	k. seen
___ 12. finally	l. found

Slowly

Swiftly

BRAVELY

From *The Basics and Beyond* © 1981, Goodyear Publishing Co., Inc.

Souvenir Shopping
(Nouns and Adjectives Review)

BUY SOME VACATION SOUVENIRS TO TAKE HOME TO YOUR FRIENDS!

★ List adjective/noun pairs for *at least ten* letters of the alphabet to identify souvenirs you might purchase on a Hawaiian vacation. (Examples: *bamboo baskets, fantastic films*)

SUPER SOUVENIRS

Adjectives	Nouns
A	
B amboo	baskets
C	
D	
E	
F	
G	
H	
I	
J	
K	
L	
M	
N	
O	
P	
Q	
R	
S	
T	
U	
V	
W	
X	
Y	
Z	

Advertising with Verbs and Adverbs

TRY YOUR LUCK! ENTER A VACATION ADVERTISING CONTEST!

★ **PART I:** Win a free scuba diving lesson by creating and writing your own advertisement, explaining why divers should use King Scuba diving equipment. Include three verbs and three adverbs in your ad, and list the verbs and adverbs you use under the ad. You may select some words from the list below, or use your own.

VERBS		ADVERBS	
dive	swim	very	often
explore	enjoy	most	easily
discover	learn	surely	certainly

OFFICIAL CONTEST ENTRY FORM

KING SCUBA*
"The Most Respected Name in Diving Equipment"

_____

_____

_____

_____

_____

_____

*Self-Contained Underwater Breathing Apparatus

VERBS	ADVERBS
1. _____	1. _____
2. _____	2. _____
3. _____	3. _____

★ **PART II:** Read the package plans advertisements below. Then fill in the information requested following the ads.

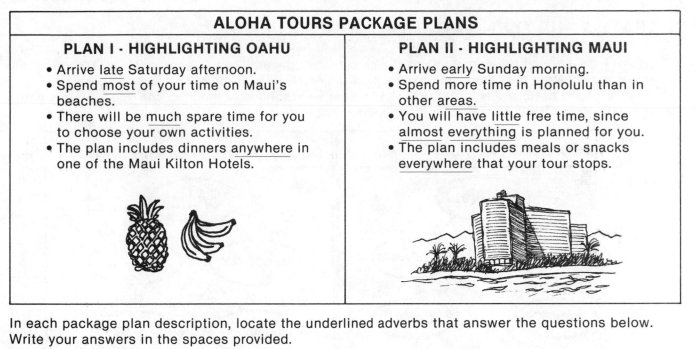

ALOHA TOURS PACKAGE PLANS

PLAN I · HIGHLIGHTING OAHU

- Arrive <u>late</u> Saturday afternoon.
- Spend <u>most</u> of your time on Maui's beaches.
- There will be <u>much</u> spare time for you to choose your <u>own</u> activities.
- The plan includes dinners <u>anywhere</u> in one of the Maui Kilton Hotels.

PLAN II · HIGHLIGHTING MAUI

- Arrive <u>early</u> Sunday morning.
- Spend <u>more</u> time in Honolulu than in other <u>areas</u>.
- You will have <u>little</u> free time, since almost <u>everything</u> is planned for you.
- The plan includes meals or snacks <u>everywhere</u> that your tour stops.

In each package plan description, locate the underlined adverbs that answer the questions below. Write your answers in the spaces provided.

	PLAN I		PLAN II
When?	1. _____	4. _____	
How Much?	2. _____	5. _____	
Where?	3. _____	6. _____	

★ **PART III:** Complete the following advertisement for a package plan by filling in appropriate adverbs that tell "when," "how much," or "where." You may choose from the following list of adverbs or use your own. (Adverbs: here, there, anywhere, nowhere, elsewhere, early, late, soon, now, then, much, some, little, least)

HIGHLIGHTING KAUAI

- Arrive _____ Monday evening.

- Spend _____ of your time on the Na Pali coast.

- The plan includes _____ of your breakfasts.

- You may dine at hotels _____ on the island.

Word Chains

CREATE YOUR OWN VACATION WORD CHAINS!

★ **PART I:** Look at the sample word chains below. Add word links to each chain by following the patterns shown. Note that one chain uses a noun/adjective word pattern, and the other uses a verb/adverb word pattern. Also note that each adjective describes or modifies the noun directly above it, and that each adverb describes or modifies the verb directly above it.

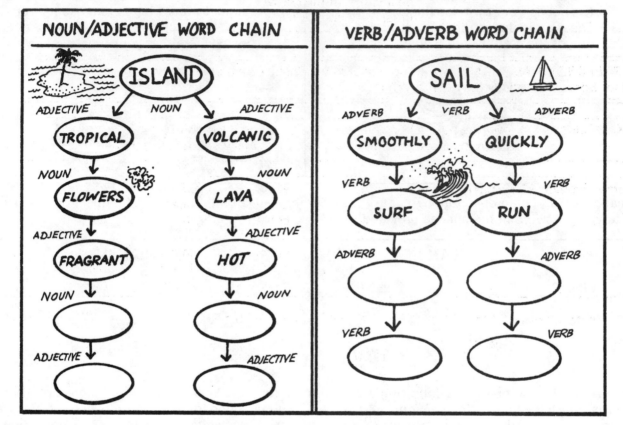

★ **PART II:** Try making your own word chains, using the patterns below.

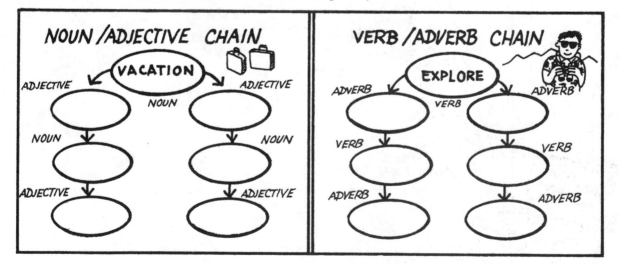

★ **PART III:** Choose any five words from the word chains above. Use the words in two or more sentences that could describe a vacation experience.

From *The Basics and Beyond* © 1981, Goodyear Publishing Co., Inc.

Dive for Prepositions

A **PREPOSITION** is a word used to show the relation of a noun or pronoun to the rest of the sentence. **PREPOSITIONS** show relations such as direction, position, and time.

EXAMPLES: The bus (noun) stopped
                       (direction)   <u>behind</u> the building
                       (position)   <u>at</u> the corner
                       (time)   <u>after</u> lunch

A **PREPOSITIONAL PHRASE** is a group of words that includes a preposition, a noun or pronoun, and other words that modify the noun or pronoun.

EXAMPLES: <u>over</u> the rickety bridge (noun)   <u>during</u> the storm (noun)
               <u>down</u> the steep path (noun)   <u>of</u> many bright colors (noun)

Some common **PREPOSITIONS** are:

up	above	around	at
down	below	near	of
on	behind	in	for
off	between	out	onto
to	under	into	after
by	over	toward	before
from	beside	with	during

TAKE A SNORKELING LESSON AND DIVE FOR PREPOSITIONS!

★ **PART I:** Underline the prepositions found in the directions below for "Snorkeling: How to Make a Surface Dive." Use the list of common prepositions to help you.

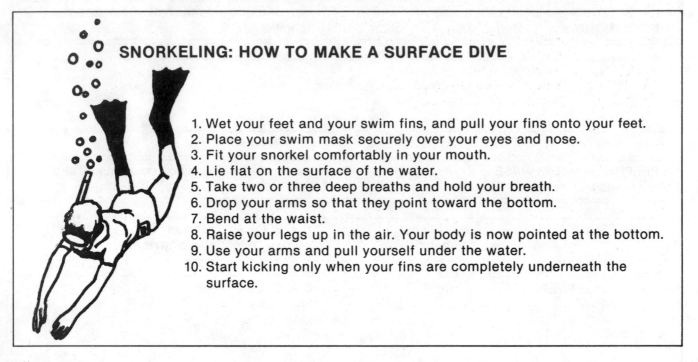

SNORKELING: HOW TO MAKE A SURFACE DIVE

1. Wet your feet and your swim fins, and pull your fins onto your feet.
2. Place your swim mask securely over your eyes and nose.
3. Fit your snorkel comfortably in your mouth.
4. Lie flat on the surface of the water.
5. Take two or three deep breaths and hold your breath.
6. Drop your arms so that they point toward the bottom.
7. Bend at the waist.
8. Raise your legs up in the air. Your body is now pointed at the bottom.
9. Use your arms and pull yourself under the water.
10. Start kicking only when your fins are completely underneath the surface.

★ **PART II:** Next to each number below, write the prepositional phrase or phrases found in the corresponding numbered statements in "Snorkeling: How To Make a Surface Dive."

1. (example) _onto your feet_

2. _____

3. _____

4. _____

   _____

5. _____ (no prepositional phrases) _____

6. _____

7. _____

8. _____

   _____

9. _____

10. _____

From *The Basics and Beyond* © 1981, Goodyear Publishing Co., Inc.

★ **PART III:** Write two or more sentences about an underwater snorkeling adventure. Include your own prepositional phrase in each sentence, or use some of the phrases given below.

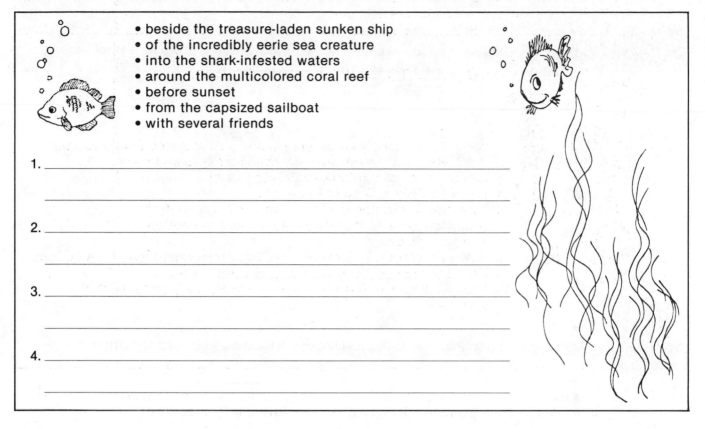

- beside the treasure-laden sunken ship
- of the incredibly eerie sea creature
- into the shark-infested waters
- around the multicolored coral reef
- before sunset
- from the capsized sailboat
- with several friends

1. _____

_____

2. _____

_____

3. _____

_____

4. _____

_____

Preposition Puzzle

★ **PART I:** Find and circle 16 different prepositions in the puzzle below. You may go across (from left to right), down, or up. (Did you notice the underlined prepositions in these puzzle directions?)

```
A P S K C L E C C T U
S B E T W E E N S L X
L E X O V E R P Q E M
V H J L A R O U N D F
X I N T O E F P I I X
Q N R U C D F O R S Y
G D D O W N T L M E O
K S R B A U A F N B N
```

PREPOSITIONS

Beside	Under
Between	Around
Up	Out
Behind	Into
On	For
In	Off
At	Down
To	Over

BONUS

★ **PART II:** Make up your own Preposition Search-A-Word Puzzle. Include at least ten different prepositions.

From *The Basics and Beyond* © 1981, Goodyear Publishing Co., Inc.

Tour with Conjunctions

A **CONJUNCTION** is a word that joins or connects thoughts, statements, or groups of words.

EXAMPLES:	Some common **CONJUNCTIONS** are:	and	but	for	nor	or	yet	unless
		both	whether	as	so	while	either	

LEARN WHAT YOUR PLANNED HAWAIIAN HOLIDAY TOUR WILL INCLUDE!

★ The sentences that follow are each missing joining words, or conjunctions. Choose the conjunctions from the list below that best connect the parts of each sentence. Write the appropriate conjunction in the spaces provided. You may only use each listed conjunction once.

CONJUNCTIONS

Unless	For	If	Or	Neither
But	While	And	Nor	Either

ALOHA TOURS

HAWAIIAN HOLIDAY—DAY 1

Begin your day enjoying a buffet breakfast at the Hawaiian Village, _____ 1 _____ your tour guide shows a film about Hawaii. Then board a bus for a tour of both downtown Honolulu _____ 2 _____ the Yacht Harbor. In the afternoon, you may _____ 3 _____ swim, surf, _____ 4 _____ browse in Waikiki. Enjoy the outdoors, _____ 5 _____ be careful not to stay too long in the hot tropical sun. Next, join your tour guide for a leisurely boat ride, _____ 6 _____ you wish. Complete your day with free hula lessons, _____ 7 _____ you would rather watch professional dancers at your hotel instead.

Remember to contact your tour guide if you have any questions, _____ 8 _____ Aloha Tours hosts and hostesses are here to serve you! We pledge to allow _____ 9 _____ poor service _____ 10 _____ careless planning to lessen your enjoyment of our island paradise!

Surf with Interjections

An **INTERJECTION** is a single word that generally expresses a strong feeling or emotion such as surprise, anger, or delight. It is usually followed by an exclamation point.

EXAMPLES: Some common **INTERJECTIONS** are: Oh!   Ouch!   Hello!   Ha!

FIND THAT PERFECT WAVE AND SURF WITH INTERJECTIONS!

★ **PART I:** Complete the following description of this surfer's experience by placing an interjection in each blank. Choose interjections from the list below. Note that several interjections may be appropriate for the same blank, so that you may select the one that most appeals to you.

INTERJECTIONS
Yow!	Hey!	Uh-oh!	Help!
Fantastic!	Nuts!	Ugh!	Whew!
Ha!	Great!	Cool!	Aha!
Well!	Look!	Oh!	Ouch!

_____! This surf is rough today. I'm paddling out slowly now to find that perfect wave. _____! This one rolling in now looks terrific! _____! I thought I'd never get up, but I made it. _____! This ride is tricky, but if the wave breaks soon, I'll be all right. _____! I wiped out, and the board just hit me on the shoulder. _____! Nothing like a mouthful of sand to complete your ride. _____! I see a fantastic breaker coming up! Look out surf, here I come again!

BONUS

★ **PART II:** Write your own description of an experience such as skateboarding, rock climbing, or playing a team sport. Write your sentences as if you were thinking them while doing the activity. Use at least five interjections in your description.

From *The Basics and Beyond* © 1981, Goodyear Publishing Co., Inc.

No Nonsense—Parts of Speech Review

INTERPRET A JOURNAL ENTRY DESCRIBING A HAWAIIAN VACATION

★ **PART I:** Note each underlined nonsense word in the following journal entry. In the numbered spaces provided, write the part of speech that each nonsense word represents. Then write an appropriate word for that part of speech, which would make the journal entry sound sensible.

Example: We <u>tringed</u> our stay in <u>gribby</u> Hawaii.
                 1   2

            1. *enjoyed: verb*   2. *sunny: adjective*

Be sure that you find at least one example of each of the eight parts of speech—noun, pronoun, verb, adjective, adverb, conjunction, preposition, interjection. (Note: You may want to review the definitions of the different parts of speech.)

HAWAIIAN JOURNAL

We flew <u>stiply</u> to <u>fribbet</u> Hawaii, where we <u>slansed</u>, <u>ferbed</u>, and <u>stoggled</u>
           1   2   3   4   5
quigley under <u>marzy</u> skies. We stayed at a modern <u>smitz</u>, and rented a <u>tollo</u> to
   6   7   8   9
make our stay more <u>zaddy</u>. Because we liked to <u>naze</u> and <u>quark</u>, Hawaii was a
           10   11   12
<u>mozzy</u> <u>graf</u> for both of <u>deme</u>. We stayed <u>zot</u> Hawaii for two weeks, and
  13   14   15   16
traveled <u>blinko</u> several islands. <u>Shazbat!</u> It couldn't have been a more
     17   18
<u>liebto</u> vacation, <u>mib</u> we plan to return someday!
  19   20

NEW WORD	PART OF SPEECH		NEW WORD	PART OF SPEECH
1. *quickly* : *adverb*		11. ____ : ____
2. ____ : ____		12. ____ : ____
3. ____ : ____		13. ____ : ____
4. ____ : ____		14. ____ : ____
5. ____ : ____		15. ____ : ____
6. ____ : ____		16. ____ : ____
7. ____ : ____		17. ____ : ____
8. ____ : ____		18. ____ : ____
9. ____ : ____		19. ____ : ____
10. ____ : ____		20. ____ : ____

BONUS

★ **PART II:** Create your own "No Nonsense" activity similar to the one in Part I. Try to write nonsense words in place of each of the eight parts of speech. Ask a friend to complete your activity.

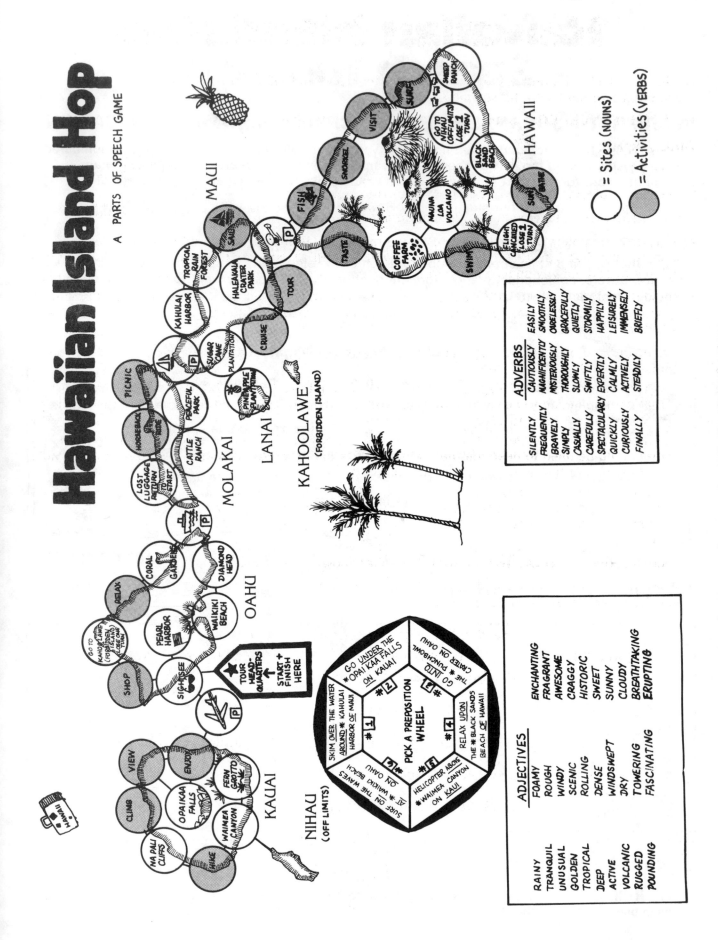

Hawaiian Island Hop

A PARTS OF SPEECH GAME

○ = Sites (NOUNS)
● = Activities (VERBS)

ADVERBS

SILENTLY	CAUTIOUSLY	EASILY
FREQUENTLY	MAGNIFICENTLY	SMOOTHLY
BRAVELY	MYSTERIOUSLY	CARELESSLY
SIMPLY	THOROUGHLY	GRACEFULLY
CASUALLY	SLOWLY	QUIETLY
CAREFULLY	SWIFTLY	STORMILY
SPECTACULARLY	EXPERTLY	HAPPILY
QUICKLY	CALMLY	LEISURELY
CURIOUSLY	ACTIVELY	IMMENSELY
FINALLY	STEADILY	BRIEFLY

PICK A PREPOSITION WHEEL

#1 SKIM OVER THE WATER AROUND * KAHULUI HARBOR OF MAUI
#2 GO UNDER THE * OPAI KAA FALLS ON KAUAI
#3 GO INTO THE * PUNCHBOWL CRATER ON OAHU
#4 RELAX UPON THE * BLACK SANDS BEACH OF HAWAII
#5 HELICOPTER ABOVE * WAIMEA CANYON ON KAUAI
#6 SURF ON THE WAVES AT * WAIKIKI BEACH ON OAHU

ADJECTIVES

FOAMY	ENCHANTING
ROUGH	FRAGRANT
WINDY	AWESOME
SCENIC	CRAGGY
ROLLING	HISTORIC
DENSE	SWEET
WINDSWEPT	SUNNY
DRY	CLOUDY
TOWERING	BREATHTAKING
FASCINATING	ERUPTING

RAINY	
TRANQUIL	
UNUSUAL	
GOLDEN	
TROPICAL	
DEEP	
ACTIVE	
VOLCANIC	
RUGGED	
POUNDING	

Board spaces include: SHEEP RANCH, SURF, VISIT, CHARCOAL, GO TO NIHAU (OFF LIMITS) LOSE 1 TURN, BLACK SAND BEACH, FISH, TASTE, MAUNA LOA VOLCANO, BATHE, HAWAII, COFFEE FARM, SWIM, SURF, FLIGHT CANCELED LOSE 1 TURN, TROPICAL RAIN FOREST, KAHULUI HARBOR, SAIL, HALEAKALA CRATER PARK, TOUR, MAUI, CRUISE, SUGAR CANE PLANTATION, PICNIC, PINEAPPLE PLANTATION, PEACEFUL PARK, HORSEBACK RIDE, CATTLE RANCH, LOST LUGGAGE RETURN TO START, MOLAKAI, LANAI, KAHOOLAWE (FORBIDDEN ISLAND), RELAX, CORAL GARDENS, DIAMOND HEAD, WAIKIKI BEACH, PEARL HARBOR, OAHU, GO TO KAHOOLAWE (FORBIDDEN ISLAND) LOSE ONE TURN, SHOP, SIGHTSEE, TOUR HEADQUARTERS, START + FINISH HERE, VIEW, ENJOY, CLIMB, OPAIKAA FALLS, FERN GROTTO, WAIMEA CANYON, NA PALI CLIFFS, HIKE, KAUAI, NIHAU (OFF LIMITS)

From *The Basics and Beyond* © 1981, Goodyear Publishing Co., Inc.

Hawaiian Island Hop

OBJECT: To be the first player to complete a tour card and return to Tour headquarters. (To complete a tour card, see the sample.)

EQUIPMENT NEEDED: Game Board, 4 Tour Cards, Die, Playing Pieces.

DIRECTIONS:

1. Pick a *TOUR CARD*.

2. Place your playing piece on *START* at "Tour Headquarters."

3. Roll the die. The player with the highest number goes first.

4. In order to complete your tour card you must move around the game board in any direction, and land on all 5 *SITES (NOUNS)* and all 5 *ACTIVITIES (VERBS)* listed on the card. You may land on your listed site and activity spaces in any order.

5. Decide which *SITE* or *ACTIVITY* space you want to go to first. Roll the die and move the number of spaces shown on the die. You do not need an *exact* roll of the die to stop on any of your *SITE* or *ACTIVITY* spaces.

6. When you land on a space listed on your tour card, check it off in the small box provided on your card. (See *SAMPLE TOUR CARD*.)

   a. When you land on a *SITE* space, choose a word from the *ADJECTIVES* list on the game board that could be used to describe that site. Write the *ADJECTIVE* on your tour card on the line next to the name of that site. (See *SAMPLE TOUR CARD*.)

   b. When you land on an *ACTIVITY* space, choose a word from the *ADVERBS* list on the game board that could be used to describe that activity. Write the *ADVERB* on your tour card on the line next to the name of that activity. (See *SAMPLE TOUR CARD*.)

   c. The other players should decide if the *ADJECTIVE* or *ADVERB* you chose is an appropriate one. If they do not accept your word, select another word from the list on the game board. Each adjective and adverb may only be used once during a game.

7. If you land on a space marked **P** (*PREPOSITION*), roll the die and follow the directions on the game board's *PREPOSITIONAL WHEEL* for the number shown on the die.

8. When you have completed your tour card, return to *TOUR HEADQUARTERS*. You must land on *FINISH* by an *exact* roll of the die to complete the game.

SAMPLE TOUR CARD (Partly Completed)

Adjectives		Sites (Nouns)	Activities (Verbs)		Adverbs
1. scenic	☑	Kauai — Fern Grotto	6. visit	☐	
2.	☐	Hawaii — Sheep Ranch	7. climb	☐	
3.	☐	Molokai — Peaceful Park	8. picnic	☑	happily
4. historic	☑	Oahu — Pearl Harbor	9. view	☐	
5.	☐	Maui — Rainforest	10. surf	☑	bravely

From *The Basics and Beyond* © 1981, Goodyear Publishing Co., Inc.

HAWAIIAN ISLAND HOP
Tour Cards
(Cut out 4 **TOUR CARDS** before playing game.)

Card 1

	ADJECTIVES	SITES (NOUNS)
1.	_____ ☐	Kauai—Fern Grotto
2.	_____ ☐	Oahu—Diamond Head
3.	_____ ☐	Molokai—Peaceful Park
4.	_____ ☐	Maui—Haleakala Crater Park
5.	_____ ☐	Hawaii—Sheep Ranch

ACTIVITIES (VERBS)	ADVERBS
1. swim	☐ _____
2. surf	☐ _____
3. horseback ride	☐ _____
4. sightsee	☐ _____
5. hike	☐ _____

Card 2

	ADJECTIVES	SITES (NOUNS)
1.	_____ ☐	Hawaii—Coffee Farm
2.	_____ ☐	Kauai—Waimea Canyon
3.	_____ ☐	Lanai—Pineapple Plantation
4.	_____ ☐	Oahu—Pearl Harbor
5.	_____ ☐	Maui—Kahulai Harbor

ACTIVITIES (VERBS)	ADVERBS
1. tour	☐ _____
2. taste	☐ _____
3. sail	☐ _____
4. shop	☐ _____
5. climb	☐ _____

Card 3

	ADJECTIVES	SITES (NOUNS)
1.	_____ ☐	Kauai—Opaikaa Falls
2.	_____ ☐	Hawaii—Mauna Loa Volcano
3.	_____ ☐	Molokai—Cattle Ranch
4.	_____ ☐	Maui—Tropical Rain Forest
5.	_____ ☐	Oahu—Coral Gardens

ACTIVITIES (VERBS)	ADVERBS
1. visit	☐ _____
2. enjoy	☐ _____
3. fish	☐ _____
4. cruise	☐ _____
5. picnic	☐ _____

Card 4

	ADJECTIVES	SITES (NOUNS)
1.	_____ ☐	Hawaii—Black Sand Beach
2.	_____ ☐	Oahu—Waikiki Beach
3.	_____ ☐	Maui—Sugar Cane Plantation
4.	_____ ☐	Molokai—Cattle Ranch
5.	_____ ☐	Kauai—Na Pali Ciffs

ACTIVITIES (VERBS)	ADVERBS
1. tour	☐ _____
2. sunbathe	☐ _____
3. snorkel	☐ _____
4. view	☐ _____
5. relax	☐ _____

From *The Basics and Beyond* © 1981, Goodyear Publishing Co., Inc.

Restaurant Review
Synonyms

SYNONYMS are words that have the same, or almost the same, meaning.

EXAMPLES: cut/slice   terrible/horrible   huge/gigantic   dish/plate

---

USE YOUR TALENTS TO REWRITE A RESTAURANT REVIEW!

★ **PART I:**   Two reporters were assigned to write a restaurant review for the Hawaiian Plain and Fancy Restaurant. Although they agreed on the excellent quality of the restaurant and the general contents of the article, they could not agree on many of the specific words in the article. In the "Restaurant Review" below, fill in the blank spaces with two synonyms that you think would be appropriate for the two reporters to consider for use in their final article.

Example: We enjoyed the (_cut_ , _sliced_) pineapple.

THE HAWAIIAN VACATIONER
"NEWS AND VIEWS OF ISLAND RECREATION"

Restaurant Review
By A. Connie Sore

The meal at the Plain and Fancy Restaurant was (_____, _____),

and we enjoyed it immensely. We began our meal with (_____, _____)

fruit. For our main course we dined on a (_____, _____) chicken dish

covered with (_____, _____) sauces. All of the dishes were served

(_____, _____) by the (_____, _____) restaurant staff.

The surroundings inside the restaurant were (_____, _____) and all

members of our family were made to feel (_____, _____) during the

meal. In addition, the meals are priced (_____, _____), which is an

additional plus for your budget. I (_____, _____) that you try the Plain

and Fancy Restaurant the next time you dine out with your family.

PLAIN & Fancy

★ **PART II:** The menu for diners at the Plain and Fancy Restaurant has two separate listings. One column lists the "plain" menu names for children (13 years and under), while the other column lists the "fancy" menu names (synonyms) for the same items. Match items from the menu by placing the letters from the "fancy" lettered items next to the appropriate numbered items in the "plain" column. Note that often phrases are used as synonyms, instead of single words.

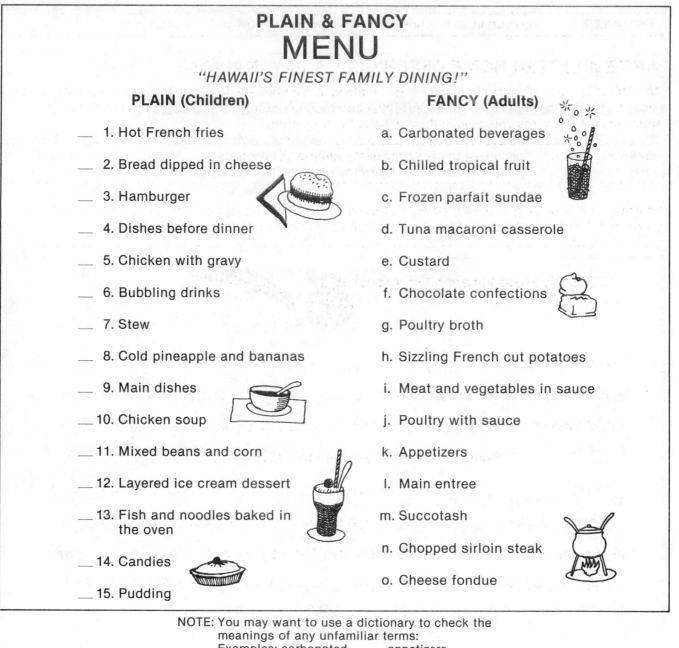

PLAIN & FANCY
MENU
"HAWAII'S FINEST FAMILY DINING!"

PLAIN (Children)	FANCY (Adults)
___ 1. Hot French fries	a. Carbonated beverages
___ 2. Bread dipped in cheese	b. Chilled tropical fruit
___ 3. Hamburger	c. Frozen parfait sundae
___ 4. Dishes before dinner	d. Tuna macaroni casserole
___ 5. Chicken with gravy	e. Custard
___ 6. Bubbling drinks	f. Chocolate confections
___ 7. Stew	g. Poultry broth
___ 8. Cold pineapple and bananas	h. Sizzling French cut potatoes
___ 9. Main dishes	i. Meat and vegetables in sauce
___ 10. Chicken soup	j. Poultry with sauce
___ 11. Mixed beans and corn	k. Appetizers
___ 12. Layered ice cream dessert	l. Main entree
___ 13. Fish and noodles baked in the oven	m. Succotash
___ 14. Candies	n. Chopped sirloin steak
___ 15. Pudding	o. Cheese fondue

NOTE: You may want to use a dictionary to check the
meanings of any unfamiliar terms:
Examples: carbonated   appetizers
          parfait   entree
          casserole   succotash
          confections   fondue
          poultry
          broth

From *The Basics and Beyond* © 1981, Goodyear Publishing Co., Inc.

Antonym Messages

ANTONYMS are words with opposite, or nearly opposite, meanings.

EXAMPLES: good/bad   hot/cold   comedy/tragedy   start/stop

WRITE A LETTER HOME DESCRIBING A DAY IN HAWAII

★ **PART I:** Complete the following letter by filling in the blanks with words that would describe a good vacation experience (Letter #1). Then, describe a bad vacation experience (Letter #2), by substituting antonyms for the words you used in the blanks of the first letter.

EXAMPLES: Today was the *best* day of my vacation. (1st letter)
Today was the *worst* day of my vacation. (2nd letter)

You may use your own antonym pairs, choosing from the antonym list that follows the letters, or find antonyms listed in a thesaurus (a reference book containing synonyms and antonyms).

LETTER #1 (Good Vacation Experience)

_____
(DATE)

Dear Aunt Nym,

Today was absolutely the most _____ day of my Hawaiian vacation.

First I took a _____ plane ride to the island of Oahu, where we visited

_____ Pearl Harbor. Next we went to a beach with huge waves that made

me feel _____. I tried surfing and _____ it. I also took a snorkeling

lesson, and was _____ by the coral reefs and tropical fish I saw. I really felt

extremely _____ under the water. The weather was _____ all

afternoon, and a _____ dinner completed my day. I hope that you

_____ have similar vacation experiences.

Fondly,

_____
(SIGNATURE)

LETTER #2 (Bad Vacation Experience)

_____
(DATE)

Dear Aunt Nym,

Today was absolutely the most _____ day of my Hawaiian vacation.

First I took a _____ plane ride to the island of Oahu, where we visited

_____ Pearl Harbor. Next we went to a beach with huge waves that made

me feel _____. I tried surfing and _____ it. I also took a snorkeling

lesson, and was _____ by the coral reefs and tropical fish I saw. I really felt

extremely _____ under the water. The weather was _____ all

afternoon, and a _____ dinner completed my day. I hope that you

_____ have similar vacation experiences.

Fondly,

_____
(SIGNATURE)

From *The Basics and Beyond* © 1981, Goodyear Publishing Co., Inc.

ANTONYM PAIRS

Fascinating/Boring   Exciting/Dull   Pleased/Disappointed   Thrilled/Disgusted   Graceful/Clumsy
Calm/Nervous   Excellent/Terrible   Never/Always   Bold/Scared   Worried/Relaxed
Brave/Cowardly   Embarrassed/Confident   Comfortable/Uncomfortable   Bumpy/Smooth
Adore/Despise   Sunny/Dreary   Sunny/Cloudy   Simple/Complex   Well/Sick

BONUS

★ **PART II:** Write another pair of similar letters, one negative and one positive, describing one of the following topics:

- The First Day of School
- A Family Vacation
- Going to Camp
- A Day at an Amusement Park
- Training a Dog

Homophone Happenings

HOMOPHONES or HOMONYMS are words that sound alike, but are spelled differently and have different meanings.

Some common HOMOPHONES are:	to/two	here/hear	there/their
(Also called HOMONYMS)	pear/pair	one/won	see/sea

WHAT'S HAPPENING? FIND OUT FROM YOUR HOTEL VACATION NEWSLETTER!

★ **PART I:** The printer of the Hawaiian Hotel Newsbreak newsletter made several errors in the final copy of the daily bulletin for guests. Correct mistakes by substituting the proper homophone for each of the underlined words in the newsletter.

HOTEL HAWAIIAN
NEPTUNE NEWSBREAK

Good *mourning* (_____₁)! *Dew* (_____₂) to the *reign* (_____₃)

yesterday, the luau was cancelled and will be held at *ate* (_____₄) o'clock this

evening, *sew* (_____₅) we hope to *sea* (_____₆) you *their* (_____₇).

Whether (_____₈) permitting, join us at the festival *sight* (_____₉)

behind the *forth* (_____₁₀) cottage. You will *here* (_____₁₁) authentic

hula music, and relax as the *read* (_____₁₂) *son* (_____₁₃) sets beyond the

shimmering *see* (_____₁₄). You'll marvel at the breathtaking view that can be *scene*

(_____₁₅) from this tropical island. *Wee* (_____₁₆) guarantee that this will be

won (_____₁₇) evening that *ewe* (_____₁₈) will never forget!

★ **PART II:**   Create your own homophone activity by writing a paragraph that contains several incorrect words. Have a friend complete the activity by replacing the incorrect words with the proper homophones. You may use your own homophones or choose some from the list below.

Flew/Flu	Do/Due/Dew	Sew/So	Stake/Steak
Sense/Cents	Course/Coarse	Bear/Bare	Sole/Soul
Poll/Pole	Through/Threw	Fare/Fair	Shoo/Shoe
Brake/Break	Meet/Meat	Stares/Stairs	Roll/Role
Sent/Scent	Know/No	Blue/Blew	Feat/Feet

HOMOPHONE HAPPENINGS

From *The Basics and Beyond* © 1981, Goodyear Publishing Co., Inc.

Compound Crosswords

A **COMPOUND WORD** is a word that is formed by joining two words that can also stand by themselves.

EXAMPLES: overhead   sunshine   upstairs
            flashlight underground

SELECT A VACATION CROSSWORD PUZZLE MAGAZINE FROM YOUR HOTEL NEWSSTAND

★ **PART I:**   Complete the vacation crossword puzzle that follows, which is made up entirely of the listed compound words or parts of compound words.

COMPOUND CROSSWORDS

ANSWERS
Choose from this list of compound words
or parts of compound words.

_____glasses   your_____
worldwide   surf_____
over_____   sail_____
foothill   suntan
sunset   air_____
horse_____   day_____
door_____   torchlight
land_____   note_____
underground   waterfall
                           _____trip

DOWN

1. Climb a small hill, or _____, at the base

of a mountain.

3. Tour Pearl Harbor, a well known site, or

_____mark.

4. Watch the sun rise at _____break.

5. Explore caves beneath the ground, or _____.

6. Ride the waves on a _____board.

7. Use _____ lotion at the beach.

9. Canoe on the rapids over a small _____.

13. Saddle up for _____back riding.

15. Stay _____night at a friend's hotel.

ACROSS

2. Travel around the world, or _____.

7. At dusk, view the scenic _____.

8. Treat _____self to a great vacation.

10. Land in your jet at the _____port.

11. Light a flaming _____ at a luau.

12. Take a round_____ cruise from Maui to

Oahu and back again.

14. Keep a diary of your vacation in a

_____book.

16. Let the tropical breezes propel your

_____boat.

17. Begin a tour from the front _____way of

your motel.

18. Wear sun_____ to protect your eyes

from the Hawaiian sun.

From *The Basics and Beyond* © 1981, Goodyear Publishing Co., Inc.

Compound Creations

COMPLETE SOME VACATION MAGAZINE ACTIVITIES USING COMPOUND WORDS

★ **PART I:** Complete the following rebus puzzle by writing the correct compound word for each numbered illustration in the following paragraph. Write your answers in the spaces provided below the rebus.

HAWAIIAN DIARY: A Day of Sailing

Today from our _____ 1 I saw a fascinating _____ 2 in the distance, and drew a

sketch of it in my _____ 3 . Later in the day I sighted a school of _____ 4 that

swam by our boat. On the way back to the island the waves became rough, and I slipped,

bumped my _____ 5 on a beam, and broke my _____ 6 . The day ended

well, though, for as we sailed into port a magnificent _____ 7 appeared in the distance.

---

1. _____   4. _____   7. _____

2. _____   5. _____

3. _____   6. _____

BONUS

★ **PART II:** Design your own rebus, using pictures for compound words. Some possible words to use are: sunlight, fishbowl, doorbell, cupcake, football, butterfly.

BONUS

★ **PART III:** Invent your own original compound words, and write a definition for each word.
   Examples: *Campcase* - a piece of luggage for carrying camping gear
   Poortour - a badly organized sightseeing trip

1. _____

2. _____

3. _____

Take Off with Affixes

An **AFFIX** is a syllable placed before or after a word (called the *root word*) to expand its meaning. A **PREFIX** is a syllable placed before a root word, and a **SUFFIX** is a syllable placed after a root word.

EXAMPLE:	*complete* (root word)	*in*complete (prefix)	complete*ly* (suffix)

Some common **PREFIXES** are:	re un in im intro dis mis pre anti super ultra fore ex non en
Some common **SUFFIXES** are:	able ly ness less ful ure ment ish ism tion ize most free al like hood

BOARD AN ALOHA AIRWAYS JET
FOR A FLIGHT WITH PREFIXES AND SUFFIXES!

★ **PART I:** All of the underlined words in the following Aloha Airways flight announcement contain affixes. List the root word, prefix, and/or suffix for each underlined word in the proper columns following the announcement. (Note: An "X" in a column indicates that no prefix or suffix appears in that word.)

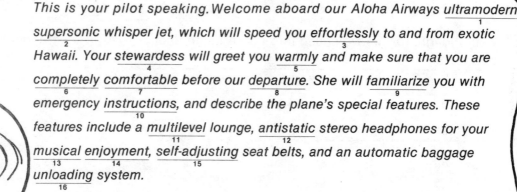

This is your pilot speaking. Welcome aboard our Aloha Airways ultramodern
supersonic whisper jet, which will speed you effortlessly to and from exotic
  2   3
Hawaii. Your stewardess will greet you warmly and make sure that you are
         4   5
completely comfortable before our departure. She will familiarize you with
  6   7   8   9
emergency instructions, and describe the plane's special features. These
         10
features include a multilevel lounge, antistatic stereo headphones for your
                 11   12
musical enjoyment, self-adjusting seat belts, and an automatic baggage
13   14   15
unloading system.
16

  Your happiness is our foremost concern on your nonstop flight to a
           17   18   19
carefree week of excitement that awaits you! Our guarantee: If you are
20   21
dissatisfied with our service, we will refund your prepaid deposit!
22   23   24

From *The Basics and Beyond* © 1981, Goodyear Publishing Co., Inc.

	PREFIX	ROOT WORD	SUFFIX
1.	ultra	modern	X
2.			X
3.	X		
4.	X		
5.	X		
6.	X		
7.	X		
8.			
9.	X		
10.	X		
11.			X
12.			X
13.	X		
14.			
15.			X
16.			X
17.	X		
18.			X
19.			X
20.	X		
21.	X		
22.			X
23.			X
24.			X

★ **PART II:** Using the list below, form five new words by adding suffixes and prefixes to the listed root words. Form at least one word that has both a prefix and a suffix. Form one word using as many prefixes and suffixes as you can.

Examples: 1. mark ──► remark ──► remarkable ──► unremarkable
2. form ──► inform

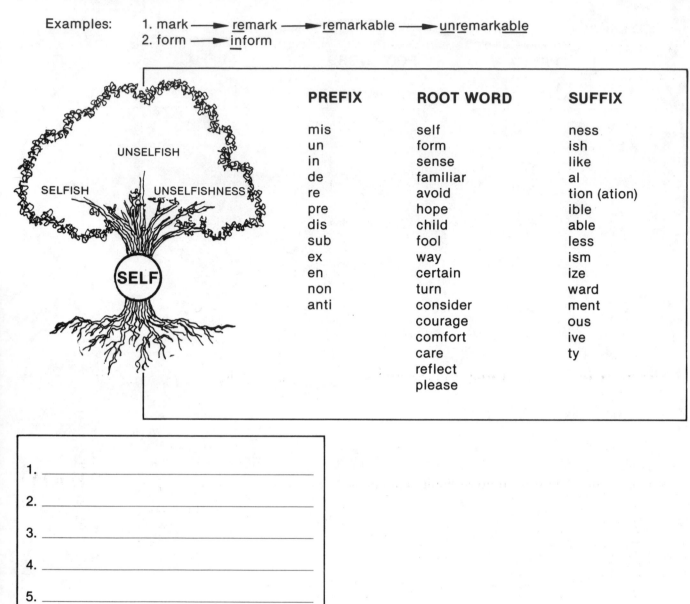

PREFIX	ROOT WORD	SUFFIX
mis	self	ness
un	form	ish
in	sense	like
de	familiar	al
re	avoid	tion (ation)
pre	hope	ible
dis	child	able
sub	fool	less
ex	way	ism
en	certain	ize
non	turn	ward
anti	consider	ment
	courage	ous
	comfort	ive
	care	ty
	reflect	
	please	

Tree labels: UNSELFISH, SELFISH, UNSELFISHNESS, SELF

From *The Basics and Beyond* © 1981, Goodyear Publishing Co., Inc.

1. _____

2. _____

3. _____

4. _____

5. _____

S E C T I O N T W O

Communicating Through the World of Sentences

SENTENCE FEATURES

NOW PLAYING

CAPITALIZATION

AND

PUNCTUATION

SENTENCE
FOUNDATIONS

★ Starring

SUBJECTS — PREDICATES
PHRASES — CLAUSES

SENTENCE FUNCTIONS
MAGAZINE

In this issue.....
STATEMENTS.
COMMANDS.
QUESTIONS?
EXCLAMATIONS!

SPECIAL EDITION
SENTENCE STRUCTURES

SIMPLE, COMPOUND, COMPLEX
SENTENCES SET WORLD
COMMUNICATION RECORD

Sentence Foundations: Subjects and Predicates

A **SENTENCE** is a group of words that expresses a complete thought and contains a **SUBJECT** and a **PREDICATE**.
- A **SUBJECT** is the part of a sentence that states about whom or what you are writing. A **COMPLETE SUBJECT** contains nouns or pronouns and related words or groups of words that describe that noun or pronoun; a **SIMPLE SUBJECT** consists of *only* the noun or pronoun.
- A **PREDICATE** is the part of a sentence that states what is being said about the subject. A **COMPLETE PREDICATE** contains verbs and other words or groups of words that relate to that verb; a **SIMPLE PREDICATE** consists of *only* the verb.

EXAMPLES:

The championship basketball team celebrated its victory.
Several thousand excited fans waited at the airport to welcome the team home.

Complete Subjects	*Complete Predicates*
The championship basketball team	celebrated its victory
Several thousand excited fans	waited at the airport to welcome the team home

Simple Subjects	*Simple Predicates*
team	celebrated
fans	waited

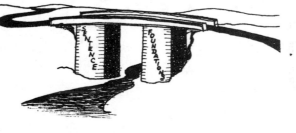

From *The Basics and Beyond* © 1981, Goodyear Publishing Co., Inc.

Football Facts

The **SIMPLE SUBJECT** of a sentence is *only* the noun or pronoun that states about whom or what you are writing.

The **SIMPLE PREDICATE** of a sentence is *only* the verb that states what is being said about the subject.

EXAMPLES: The challenging <u>Redskins</u>   <u>stopped</u>   the sluggish Eagles.
                        (SIMPLE SUBJECT) (SIMPLE PREDICATE)

               The angry   <u>coach</u>   <u>shouted</u>   loudly at several players.
                        (SIMPLE SUBJECT) (SIMPLE PREDICATE)

BECOME AN INFORMED FAN AND FIND OUT WHAT'S BEEN HAPPENING IN THE NATIONAL FOOTBALL LEAGUE

★ **PART I:**   Using the "Football Headlines Around the League," find the *simple subject* and the *simple predicate* in each headline. Place the simple subject and the simple predicate for each numbered headline in the correct columns below.

SIMPLE SUBJECT   **SIMPLE PREDICATE**

1. _____   _____

2. _____   _____

3. _____   _____

4. _____   _____

5. _____   _____

6. _____   _____

7. _____   _____

8. _____   _____

9. _____   _____

10. _____   _____

① **Redskins Hold Off Eagles**

② *Rams Blank Falcons for 2nd Victory*

③ **Jets Edge Bills**

④ *Campbell Leads Oilers*

⑤ ***Dolphins Rip Colts, 42-0***

⑥ **Bears Sink 49ers**

⑦ **Bengals Beat Browns On Overtime Field Goal**

⑧ *Cardinals Beaten by Pats, 16-6*

⑨ ***Whitehurst Bombs Saints***

⑩ **Vikings Host Broncos Tonight**

★ **PART II:** As a sports editor, you have received the following scores over the ticker tape machine. Make up your own headlines using the game scores, and place them in the "Sports Edition" space below. Underline the simple subject and circle the simple predicate for each headline.

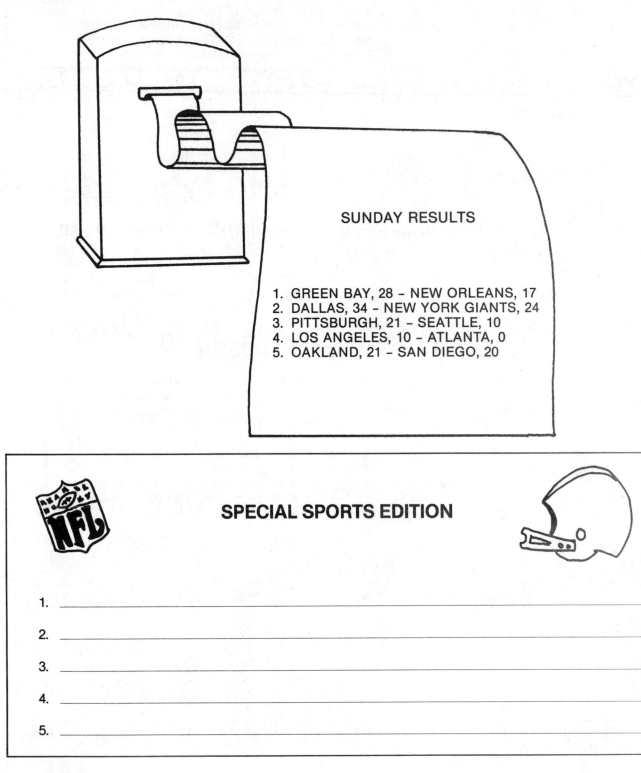

SUNDAY RESULTS

1. GREEN BAY, 28 – NEW ORLEANS, 17
2. DALLAS, 34 – NEW YORK GIANTS, 24
3. PITTSBURGH, 21 – SEATTLE, 10
4. LOS ANGELES, 10 – ATLANTA, 0
5. OAKLAND, 21 – SAN DIEGO, 20

SPECIAL SPORTS EDITION

1. _____
2. _____
3. _____
4. _____
5. _____

BONUS

★ **PART III:** Clip five to ten headlines from your local newspaper. Underline all of the simple subjects; circle all of the simple predicates.

From *The Basics and Beyond* © 1981, Goodyear Publishing Co., Inc.

Tennis Topics

The **COMPLETE SUBJECT** of a sentence contains a noun or pronoun, and often includes related words or groups of words that describe the noun or pronoun. The **COMPLETE PREDICATE** of a sentence contains a verb, and often includes other words or groups of words that relate to that verb.

EXAMPLES:

Complete Subjects	Complete Predicates
The famous tennis player	won an exciting match.
You	watched the match with a friend.
A large crowd of spectators	applauded wildly.

GET ON THE BALL! USE TENNIS NEWSPAPER ARTICLES TO HELP YOU SWING INTO LOCATING COMPLETE SUBJECTS AND PREDICATES!

★ **PART I:** Find the *complete subject* for each numbered sentence in the newspaper story below. Write the *complete subjects* in the spaces provided following the story. (Note: The complete subject may be one word or several words.)

SEVERT SWINGS BY TOSSIN 🎾

(1) Liz Severt, America's tennis queen, scored a victory in the U.S. Open over Stacy Tossin, the young 16-year-old newcomer. (2) The two-handed backhand player, Severt, won against Tossin on the clay court in straight sets. (3) The two women have played five times in the past year. (4) Their scores are getting closer with each match.

(5) Stacy Tossin, who has been referred to in the past as Stacy in Wonderland, was the youngest player ever to compete in the U.S. Open. (6) She might have done better in this match by coming to the net more often against her opponent.

(7) The tennis challenger of the future, Tossin, is growing stronger every year, and represents a real threat to Severt. (8) Soon Severt will not be swinging by Tossin that often.

COMPLETE SUBJECTS

1. Liz Severt, America's tennis queen
2. _____
3. _____
4. _____
5. _____
6. _____
7. _____
8. _____

From *The Basics and Beyond* © 1981, Goodyear Publishing Co., Inc.

★ **PART II:** Find the complete predicate for each numbered sentence in the newspaper ad below. Write the complete predicates in the numbered spaces following the ad.

SUPERTOES TENNIS SHOES

(1) You can keep on your toes, run faster, and stay out in front with Supertoes Tennis Shoes. (2) They help you keep your balance and give you a better chance to win the game. (3) These shoes, designed to last longer than many others, are made of durable materials. (4) Boys, girls, men, and women will all enjoy staying in shape and exercising with Supertoes Tennis Shoes.

ADVERTISEMENT

COMPLETE PREDICATES

1. _____

2. _____

3. _____

4. _____

BONUS

★ **PART III:** Find and clip a paragraph from a newspaper sports article. Paste your paragraph in the space below. After reading the article, list the complete subject and underline the complete predicate of each sentence.

From *The Basics and Beyond* © 1981, Goodyear Publishing Co., Inc.

Confused News

A **PHRASE** is a group of words that is not a complete sentence. It does not contain both a subject and a predicate.

EXAMPLES:		
in the newspaper		as the headlines said
when the reporter		for today's news
an eyewitness account		answering the questions

REPORT SOME NEWS FOR THE "CONFUSED NEWS GAZETTE"

★ **PART I:** Imagine that you are a reporter for the "Confused News Gazette." Write five opening sentences (called "leads") for humorous confused news stories by: (1) choosing one phrase at random from each column below, and (2) combining the phrases to form each lead sentence.

EXAMPLES:	WHO	WHAT	WHERE	WHEN
	Several area teachers	*struck oil*	*in a circus tent*	*during lunch.*

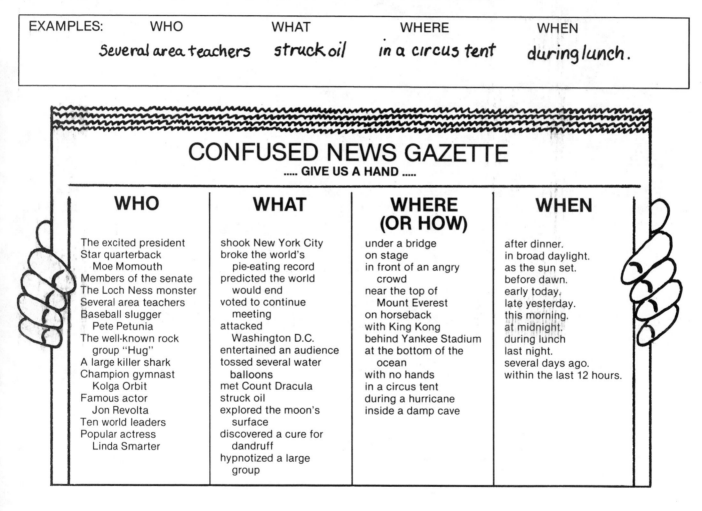

CONFUSED NEWS GAZETTE
..... GIVE US A HAND .....

WHO	WHAT	WHERE (OR HOW)	WHEN
The excited president	shook New York City	under a bridge	after dinner.
Star quarterback Moe Momouth	broke the world's pie-eating record	on stage	in broad daylight.
Members of the senate	predicted the world would end	in front of an angry crowd	as the sun set.
The Loch Ness monster	voted to continue meeting	near the top of Mount Everest	before dawn.
Several area teachers	attacked Washington D.C.	on horseback	early today.
Baseball slugger Pete Petunia	entertained an audience	with King Kong	late yesterday.
The well-known rock group "Hug"	tossed several water balloons	behind Yankee Stadium	this morning.
A large killer shark	met Count Dracula	at the bottom of the ocean	at midnight.
Champion gymnast Kolga Orbit	struck oil	with no hands	during lunch
Famous actor Jon Revolta	explored the moon's surface	in a circus tent	last night.
Ten world leaders	discovered a cure for dandruff	during a hurricane	several days ago.
Popular actress Linda Smarter	hypnotized a large group	inside a damp cave	within the last 12 hours.

From *The Basics and Beyond* © 1981, Goodyear Publishing Co., Inc.

1. _____

2. _____

3. _____

4. _____

5. _____

★ **PART II:** Write a short confused news story (one paragraph) to explain or expand one of the "lead" sentences that you created in PART I. Also write a headline for your story.

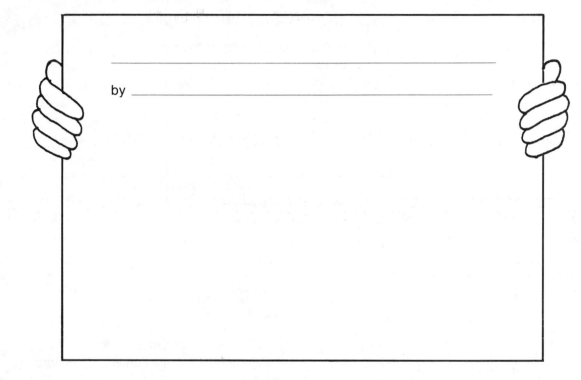

by _____

★ **PART III:** Create four or five sets of phrases, using the form below. (You might ask a friend to use your phrases to write some "confused news" sentences.)

	WHO	WHAT	WHERE (OR HOW)	WHEN
1.				
2.				
3.				
4.				
5.				

Video Phrases

JOIN THE NETWORKS IN PREVIEWING TELEVISION'S NEW SUPER SEASON!

★ **PART I:** Using the phrases below about new television programs listed in *TV Viewing* Magazine, write one or two sentences describing any four of those programs. Place your sentences in the illustrated television screens that follow. If you wish, you may add some phrases of your own to the information given about each program.

EXAMPLE:

MYSTERY:
SHERLOCK + FRIENDS

For amateur detectives;
suspenseful & intriguing;
solutions to mysteries
offered by viewers.

WATCH SHERLOCK & FRIENDS,
THE NEW MYSTERY SHOW FOR
AMATEUR DETECTIVES. THE
PROGRAM PRESENTS SUSPENSE-
FUL AND INTRIGUING TALES,
IN WHICH THE VIEWER HELPS
TO SOLVE MYSTERIES.

TV VIEWING
SUPER SEASON!
... PREVIEW OF NEW PROGRAMS ...

Tune-in to a Super Season!

HISTORY: "It's About Time"
Time travel to the past by a group of friends; participation by travelers in actual historical events.

★ **GAME SHOW: "Reach for the Stars"**
Questions asked about TV, movies, and performers; chances for winning contestants to interview favorite stars; films of winners and stars spending a day together.

ADVENTURE: "Galaxy Nova"
Exciting adventures in a far-off galaxy; control of humans by robot society; attempts to colonize other worlds.

SPORTS: "The Name of the Game"
How popular team sports were developed; stories about sports personalities; tips on how to improve skills.

COMEDY: "Far Out!"
Community life in a space station; lots of laughs; rib-tickling situations; humorous characters.

VARIETY: "Talent U.S.A."
Broadcast from a different city each week; performances by local talent in music and comedy.

SCIENCE: "Animal Days and Ways"
Fascinating facts about the animal world; rare films of endangered species; visits to all of the world's continents and oceans.

NEWS: "Kids in the News"
Comments by kids on news stories of interest to young people; consumer reports on kids' products; focus on kids in the community.

From *The Basics and Beyond* © 1981, Goodyear Publishing Co., Inc.

Title:

Title:

Title:

Title:

★ **PART II:** Create your own television show. Write the title of the show and some phrases to explain it. Then write a description of the program, using complete sentences.

_____

_____

_____

_____

_____

_____

Phrase-a-Product

PROMOTE SOME PRODUCTS! FIND AND USE PHRASES TO CREATE UNIQUE ADVERTISEMENTS

★ **PART I:** The "Alert Advertiser" contains an ad for the product described below. After reading the ad that follows match the Product Phrases with the correct numbered spaces found in the advertisement. Write the number next to each listed product phrase.

THE KITTEN'S MEOW

Did you know that kittens grow from babies _____ in only
                                                          1

a year? While they are growing they need extra nutrition,

_____ and extra minerals. They need extra vitamins for
          2

shiny coats and keen bright eyes. They need extra minerals for

_____ and strong bones. Help your kitten grow in a healthy
          3

way by purchasing The Kitten's Meow cat food, available _____.
                                                                    4

Let your kitten chow down with The Kitten's Meow.

PRODUCT PHRASES
____including extra
        vitamins
____to adult cats
____from any grocery
      store near you
____strong teeth

★ **PART II:** You are an advertising agent. Choose any three products from your account list below, and write some phrases describing the product. Write your phrases in the boxes provided.

Example:
- mouth-watering taste
- tingles the tongue

Winners/Losers

A **CLAUSE** is a group of words (within a sentence) that contains a subject (noun or pronoun) and a predicate (verb) of its own. A **CLAUSE** that does not express a complete thought and cannot stand alone as a sentence is called an **INDEPENDENT CLAUSE**. A **CLAUSE** that does not express a complete thought and cannot stand alone as a sentence is called a **DEPENDENT CLAUSE** (it depends on the rest of the sentence for its meaning).

EXAMPLES:

simple subject
simple predicate

- A suspect had been arrested   (independent clause)
    when the reporter arrived on the scene.   (dependent clause)
- Since a group of bystanders had witnessed the crime,   (dependent clause)
    the reporter interviewed several people.   (independent clause)
- The reporter filed her story with the news editor,   (independent clause)
    after she completed her interviews.   (dependent clause)

SUBMIT YOUR IDEAS TO GROOVE MAGAZINE NOW!

★ Next month's issue of **Groove** Magazine is featuring a column called "Winners" and "Losers," based on ideas sent in by readers. After reading the directions and examples that follow, write three ideas for both the "Winners" and "Losers" columns. To complete the unfinished sentences in each column, add a dependent clause to each listed independent clause. Begin each clause that you write with the conjunction "when."

From *The Basics and Beyond* © 1981, Goodyear Publishing Co., Inc.

Groove

Dear Reader,

Was your day today a **winner** or a **loser**? Look at the samples below and then send us your ideas. We'll select the best entries to print in next month's magazine.

        Thanks,
        The Editors

SAMPLES

You know your day is a **winner** . . .
    (independent clause)

when you put a quarter in a vending machine and get two drinks. (dependent clause)

You know your day is a **loser** . . .
    (independent clause)

when you get all dressed up for a party and everyone else comes in wearing jeans. (dependent clause)

WINNERS

You know your day is a **winner** . . .

1. when_____

   _____

2. when _____

   _____

3. when _____

   _____

LOSERS

You know your day is a **loser** . . .

1. when_____

   _____

2. when _____

   _____

3. when _____

   _____

Editors' Note: You may illustrate two of your ideas in the spaces provided above, if you wish.

Get in the Groove

WRITE AN AD FOR *GROOVE* MAGAZINE!

★ **Groove** Magazine has invited its readers to help write ads to promote the magazine. Complete the statements below by adding an independent clause to each given dependent clause. Make sure that each clause you write could stand alone as a sentence.

Groove

Dear Reader,

Get in the **Groove**! Look at the sample below and then write your own ad for **Groove**! If your idea is selected to be used for advertising, you will receive a free one-year subscription to our magazine.

SAMPLE: Although **Groove** only costs 50¢ (dependent clause)
it's worth its weight in gold! (independent clause)

1. Because **Groove** is the magazine for those who think young,

_____!

2. Unless you subscribe to **Groove**

_____!

3. When you read **Groove**

_____!

4. Wherever you find a copy of **Groove**

_____!

5. _____

while **Groove** is around!

6. _____

after **Groove** arrives!

GET IN THE GROOVE!

groove

THE MAGAZINE FOR THOSE WHO THINK YOUNG !!!

From *The Basics and Beyond* © 1981, Goodyear Publishing Co., Inc.

Sentence Structure

A **SIMPLE SENTENCE** is a group of words that expresses one main idea or complete thought and contains a subject and a predicate.

(Note: In all examples that follow, the simple subjects of sentences are underlined once, the simple predicates are underlined twice, and the conjunctions used to join the clauses are circled.)

EXAMPLES:
1. The singer crooned a sad song.
2. The audience listened silently.
3. The television show was exciting.
4. You dozed in front of the TV set.

A **COMPOUND SENTENCE** is a group of words that combines two or more main ideas or complete thoughts. Each thought (independent clause) contains a subject and a predicate and can stand alone as a sentence. The parts (independent clauses) of a **COMPOUND** sentence are joined by conjunctions such as: and, but, or, nor, yet.

EXAMPLES:
1. The singer crooned a sad song, and the audience listened silently.
2. The television show was exciting, but you dozed in front of the TV set.

A **COMPLEX SENTENCE** is a group of words that expresses two main ideas. One idea (an independent clause) expresses a complete thought, and can stand alone as a sentence. The other idea (a dependent clause) does not express a complete thought, and cannot stand alone as a sentence (it depends on the rest of the sentence for its meaning). The two parts (clauses) of a **COMPLEX SENTENCE** each contain a subject and a predicate, and are joined by conjunctions such as: after, although, as, because, before, if, since, though, unless, until, when, while.

EXAMPLES:
1. The singer crooned a sad song,   (independent clause)
   while the audience listened silently.   (dependent clause)
2. Although the television show was exciting,   (dependent clause)
   you dozed in front of the TV set.   (independent clause)

From *The Basics and Beyond* © 1981, Goodyear Publishing Co., Inc.

Comedy Corner

COLLECT SOME JOKES FOR *GROOVE* MAGAZINE'S COMEDY CORNER!

★ **PART I:** **Groove** has asked you to submit some jokes for the magazine's Comedy Corner column. Combine parts of jokes by matching the following riddle questions with their answers (called "punch lines"). Place the letter of the correct punch line beside each numbered question. Then, write five *simple sentences*, using any five of the jokes.

EXAMPLES:

<u>b</u> 1. What is yellow and tough and carries a silver bullet?

<u>a</u> 2. What is green and goes click click?

    a. A ball point pickle

    b. The Lone Banana

1. The Lone Banana is yellow and tough and carries a silver bullet.
2. A ball point pickle is green and goes click click.

___ 1. What is yellow, noisy, and very dangerous?

___ 2. What is red and has bucket seats?

___ 3. What is huge, hairy, and plays table tennis?

___ 4. What is purple and plugs in?

___ 5. What is juicy and stamps out forest fires?

___ 6. What is wrinkled and goes slam slam?

___ 7. What is purple and wants to conquer the world?

___ 8. What is yellow and flies great distances?

___ 9. What is red and goes putt putt?

___ 10. What is green and able to leap tall buildings in a single bound?

a. Smokey the Grape

b. Superpickle

c. King Pong

d. a thundering herd of lemons

e. a two-door prune

f. an outboard radish

g. Alexander the Grape

h. a foreign sports apple

i. an electric grape

j. an intercontinental banana missile

1. _____

2. _____

3. _____

4. _____

5. _____

From *The Basics and Beyond* © 1981, Goodyear Publishing Co., Inc.

★ **PART II:** Write five *simple sentences* in the form of questions by creating riddles for any of the "punch lines" below. Place the letter of the correct punch line next to each riddle question that you write.

EXAMPLE:	Punch Line – Sherlock Zebra
	Question – What is black and white and solves crimes?

PUNCH LINES

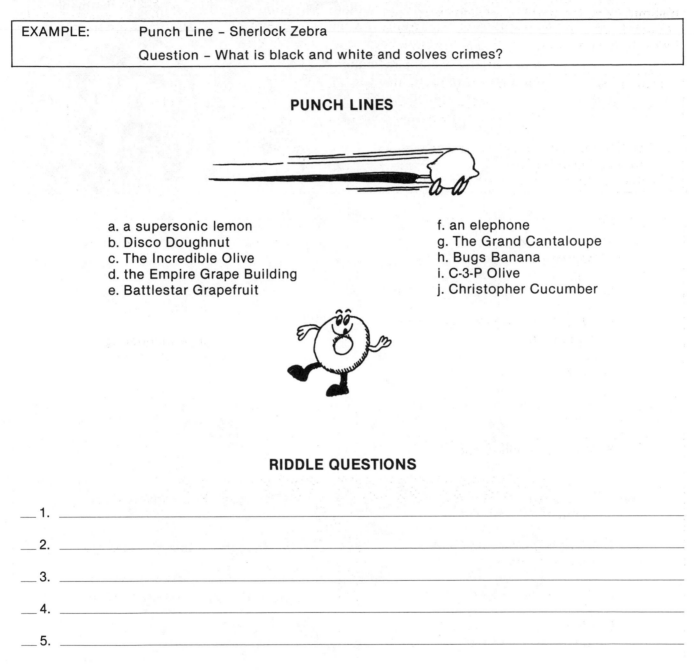

a. a supersonic lemon
b. Disco Doughnut
c. The Incredible Olive
d. the Empire Grape Building
e. Battlestar Grapefruit

f. an elephone
g. The Grand Cantaloupe
h. Bugs Banana
i. C-3-P Olive
j. Christopher Cucumber

RIDDLE QUESTIONS

___ 1. _____

___ 2. _____

___ 3. _____

___ 4. _____

___ 5. _____

Button Messages

ENJOY *GROOVE* MAGAZINE'S COLLECTION OF MESSAGE BUTTONS!

★ **PART I:** Unscramble each button message below to form *simple sentences.* Choose three of your sentences and place them in the button outlines. Write the correct sentences in the blanks provided. You may design these buttons any way you wish.

> EXAMPLES: blood in invest Vampires banks
>   Vampires invest in blood banks.
> NOTE: First words of messages are capitalized.

1. bite nails Carpenters their shouldn't

   _____

2. class all have Teachers

   _____

3. uncommon Skunks scents have

   _____

4. in House the and in Senate the A place woman's is

   _____

5. life kick of out get players Soccer a

   _____

6. are Quarterbacks ball the on

   _____

7. pits Prunes the are really

   _____

8. par up are to Golfers

   _____

9. are this Astronauts of out world

   _____

10. for worked Carter peanuts ex-President

   _____

★ **PART II:** Create your own message or messages for a button or buttons that you might want to wear. Use a simple sentence for each button message.

   _____

From *The Basics and Beyond* © 1981, Goodyear Publishing Co., Inc.

Compound Captions

A **COMPOUND SENTENCE** is a group of words that combines two or more main ideas or complete thoughts. Each thought contains a subject and a predicate.

CREATE YOUR OWN COMPOUND SENTENCE CAPTIONS

★ **PART I:** Complete the captions for each frame of the comic strip below by writing a compound sentence that gives "good news" in the first part of the sentence, and "bad news" in the second part of the sentence. Use the conjunction "but" to connect the two parts of your sentences. Remember, each part of your compound sentence must be able to stand alone as a complete sentence.

GOOD NEWS | **BAD NEWS**

You've learned how to fly a plane, | **but** The plane runs out of gas!

Luckily, you brought a parachute, | **but**

?

Fortunately, | **but**

★ **PART II:** Create two good news/bad news comics, using your own drawings and writing compound sentences for the captions. Choose your own topic, or select a topic from the suggestions below.

You won $5,000 in a contest, but . . .
You were chosen to star in a play, but . . .
You received a new bike for your birthday, but . . .

GOOD NEWS	**BAD NEWS**

You   but

GOOD NEWS	**BAD NEWS**

You   but

★ **PART III:** Write a *compound sentence* caption giving information about each of the four Supershine Line products pictured above. Use one of the following conjunctions to join the two parts of each compound sentence: *and, or, but.*

EXAMPLE: Shiny Shampoo is guaranteed to make your hair shiny, *or* you get your money back.

1. Shiny Shampoo makes a lot of lather, _____

2. _____

3. _____

4. _____

Complex Copy

A **COMPLEX SENTENCE** is a group of words that expresses two main ideas. One idea (independent clause) expresses a complete thought, and can stand alone as a sentence. The other idea (dependent clause) does not express a complete thought, and cannot stand alone as a sentence.

HELP A NEWSPAPER REPORTER COMPLETE THE FINAL COPY FOR THE EVENING EDITION!

★ A newspaper reporter used notecards to jot down information about a fire for a news story. Help the reporter form complex sentences for the story by correctly matching the dependent and independent clauses from the notecards below. Place the letter of the correct clause from Card #2 next to the matching clause from Card #1.

Card #1   *Rain Could Put a Wet Blanket on California Fire*
(Independent Clauses)

___ 1. A raging fire spread throughout a suburb of Los Angeles, California, today,…

___ 2. It is believed that the fire was started by a careless smoker,…

___ 3. Two hundred residents were safely evacuated from their houses,…

___ 4. Hundreds of volunteers helped set up emergency shelters,…

___ 5. Tons of water and chemicals have been dumped on the raging fire by air,…

___ 6. _____,
the fire could be under control by the weekend.

Card #2   *Rain Could Put a Wet Blanket on California Fire*
(Dependent Clauses)

a. when they were alerted by rescue workers.

b. If the heavy rains come tomorrow as predicted.

c. because of a severe drought that had existed for several weeks.

d. although in some areas the smoke was too dense for the use of airplanes.

e. where they brought cots and food.

f. although the exact cause of the fire is still unknown.

From *The Basics and Beyond* © 1981, Goodyear Publishing Co., Inc.

Complex Cop-Outs

**APPLY FOR THE "BEST EXCUSE OF THE YEAR" AWARD
BY ENTERING *GROOVE* MAGAZINE'S COMPLEX COP-OUT CONTEST!**

★ **PART I:** Write five complex sentences by making up your own excuses for the following situations. Use the conjunctions *because, since,* or *unless* in completing your complex sentences.

EXAMPLE: 	Why I can't eat the unwrapped chocolate candy bar you just took out of your pocket and gave to me: I can't eat this terrific candy bar you gave me because I break out in red blotches when I eat chocolate.

1. Why I can't go to the dentist this Saturday:

I can't go to the dentist this Saturday because _____

_____

2. Why I can't go to the family reunion at Aunt Louella's house:

_____

_____

3. Why I can't pay back the money I owe my friend:

_____

_____

4. Why I can't eat the spinach-raisin casserole my mom spent hours making for dinner:

_____

_____

5. Why I can't clean my room for a week:

_____

_____

★ **PART II:** Create your own situation and write a cop-out excuse for that situation. Use a complex sentence when writing your excuse. You may illustrate your "cop-out" if you wish.

Situation: _____

Cop-out: _____

_____

TV Talk: State Your Sentence

TYPES OF SENTENCES

A **DECLARATIVE SENTENCE (STATEMENT)** is one that makes a statement. It ends with a period.

A **INTERROGATIVE SENTENCE (QUESTION)** is one that asks a question. It ends with a question mark.

An **IMPERATIVE SENTENCE (COMMAND)** is one that gives a command or makes a request. It ends with a period.

An **EXCLAMATORY SENTENCE (EXCLAMATION)** is one that expresses surprise or strong feelings. It ends with an exclamation point!

Examples:

STATEMENT: Battlestar Galactica is a television science fiction show.

QUESTION: Did you watch Battlestar Galactica this week?

COMMAND: Turn on the TV and watch Battlestar Galactica.

EXCLAMATION: The last episode of Battlestar Galactica was great!

TAKE PART IN A TELEVISION INTERVIEW AND HELP WRITE A TV SCRIPT!

★ **PART I:** Read over the definitions of the types of sentences and then read the following interview. In the spaces provided, write the letter of the correct type of sentence next to each viewer's response (S = Statement, Q = Question, C = Command, E = Exclamation).

TV ANNOUNCER: "You may recall that Battlestar Galactica follows the adventures of a group of survivors of an advanced human civilization who are fleeing from another galaxy. Many hostile beings pursue these adventurers. Today we are going to listen to some recorded responses from interviews with our television viewers about this show."

VIEWERS:

___ 1. "Battlestar Galactica is a good show, and I watch it a lot."

___ 2. "Are you really calling from a TV station?"

___ 3. "My favorite show was when Starbuck crashed on another planet."

___ 4. "Make each show last longer."

___ 5. "What a terrific show!"

___ 6. "Is this show a take-off on Star Wars?"

★ **PART II:** Write four sentences below, using the four types of sentences. Write your sentences as if you were a television viewer being interviewed about the show, Battlestar Galactica, or about one of your own favorite shows.

STATEMENT: _____

QUESTION: _____

COMMAND: _____

EXCLAMATION: _____

★ **PART III:** A television writer was asked to prepare a script for a show called "Program Previews" describing some upcoming television shows. Help the writer include a variety of sentence types in the script by changing the statements below to either *questions, commands,* or *exclamations.* Use all three types of sentences, and identify the type of sentence you wrote. Place all of your responses in the "Rewrite" spaces provided.

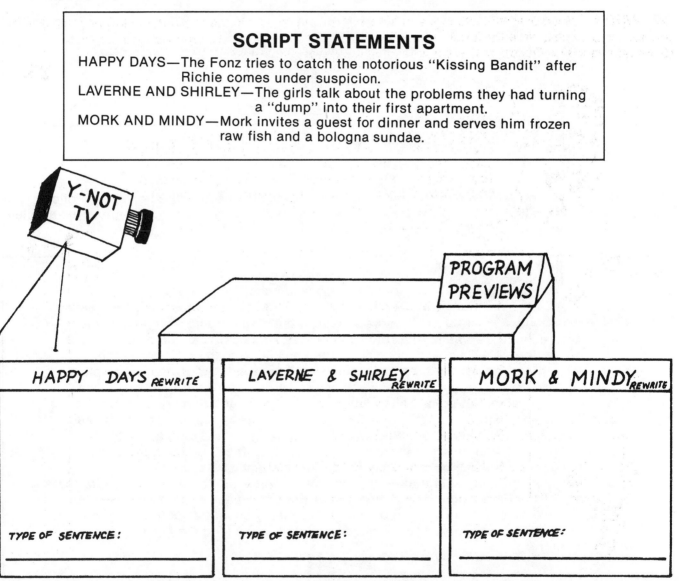

SCRIPT STATEMENTS

HAPPY DAYS—The Fonz tries to catch the notorious "Kissing Bandit" after Richie comes under suspicion.

LAVERNE AND SHIRLEY—The girls talk about the problems they had turning a "dump" into their first apartment.

MORK AND MINDY—Mork invites a guest for dinner and serves him frozen raw fish and a bologna sundae.

Y-NOT TV

PROGRAM PREVIEWS

HAPPY DAYS REWRITE	LAVERNE & SHIRLEY REWRITE	MORK & MINDY REWRITE
TYPE OF SENTENCE:	TYPE OF SENTENCE:	TYPE OF SENTENCE:

Correct Capitals

From *The Basics and Beyond* © 1981, Goodyear Publishing Co., Inc.

> **CAPITALIZATION** is the use of written capital letters for specific words or uses of words.

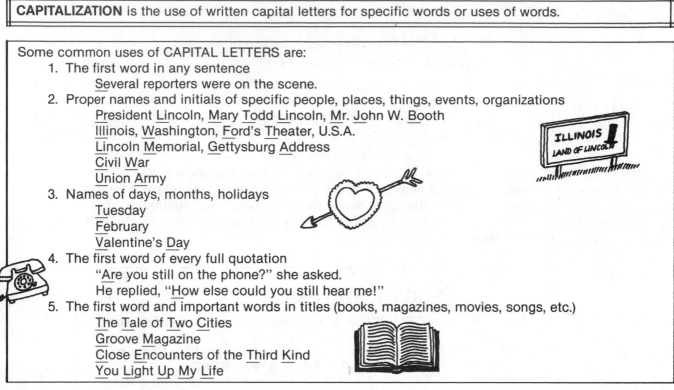

Some common uses of CAPITAL LETTERS are:

1. The first word in any sentence
   <u>S</u>everal reporters were on the scene.
2. Proper names and initials of specific people, places, things, events, organizations
   <u>P</u>resident <u>L</u>incoln, <u>M</u>ary <u>T</u>odd <u>L</u>incoln, <u>M</u>r. <u>J</u>ohn <u>W</u>. <u>B</u>ooth
   <u>I</u>llinois, <u>W</u>ashington, <u>F</u>ord's <u>T</u>heater, <u>U</u>.<u>S</u>.<u>A</u>.
   <u>L</u>incoln <u>M</u>emorial, <u>G</u>ettysburg <u>A</u>ddress
   <u>C</u>ivil <u>W</u>ar
   <u>U</u>nion <u>A</u>rmy
3. Names of days, months, holidays
   <u>T</u>uesday
   <u>F</u>ebruary
   <u>V</u>alentine's <u>D</u>ay
4. The first word of every full quotation
   "<u>A</u>re you still on the phone?" she asked.
   He replied, "<u>H</u>ow else could you still hear me!"
5. The first word and important words in titles (books, magazines, movies, songs, etc.)
   <u>T</u>he <u>T</u>ale of <u>T</u>wo <u>C</u>ities
   <u>G</u>roove <u>M</u>agazine
   <u>C</u>lose <u>E</u>ncounters of the <u>T</u>hird <u>K</u>ind
   <u>Y</u>ou <u>L</u>ight <u>U</u>p <u>M</u>y <u>L</u>ife

CAPITALIZE A FEATURE NEWS STORY REPORTED BY THE SPEEDY WIRE SERVICE

★ **PART I:** Your newsroom has just received a story over the Speedy Wire Service—"Police Uncover Masked Bandit." All capital letters have been omitted from the report. Proofread the article and circle each word that should be capitalized.

 police uncover masked bandit

speedy wire service

on friday, january 8th, at the nine corners medical building in funfax, virginia, doctor ivan ben taken's office was burglarized. on saturday, dr. taken changed all of the locks on his office doors. however, the burglar was not easily discouraged. sunday morning dr. taken's office was again found in shambles, and another burglary had taken place. when interviewed, dr. ivan b. taken said, "these burglaries really surprise me. only a few pills are missing, but so much is broken and ruined. i can't think of anyone who would want to do this to me." that sunday night the funfax police department staked out the office. no one was seen either entering or leaving the building all night. however, on monday morning it was discovered that the office had been ransacked again. finally the mystery was solved and the masked bandit was captured. at this moment dr. taken finally said that he felt safe, and that he would no longer require the protection of the funfax police department. a raccoon had been entering the building through a heating duct! our system of justice had mercy upon the suspect and returned the accused raccoon to the woods in his own custody. so ended the mystery of the masked bandit.

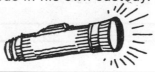

★ **PART II:** The Capitalization Chart below lists five rules for capitalizing words. List all of the circled words from the "Police Uncover Masked Bandit" article under the correct heading (rule). (Note: some words may be listed under more than one heading.)

CAPITALIZATION CHART
Rules for Capitalizing Words

A First Word in a Sentence	B Proper Names of Places, People, Groups	C Names of Days, Months	D Titles	E First Word of a Quotation

Capitalize on This

PROOFREAD A MAGAZINE ARTICLE AND LOCATE CAPITALIZED WORDS

★ **PART I:** The capital shift key on the typewriter was not working when a reporter wrote the following article. In the numbered spaces following each column in the article, write each word that should be capitalized.

"PROUD PARENTS AND CUDDLY CUBS"

the black bears, teddy and sarah, keep cool in a shaded cage at the newburg zoo. in the early spring a pair of cubs was born. the zoo keeper, mr. joseph r. bars, who raised both adult bears, returned immediately from his vacation in dallas, texas, when he heard about the birth of the cubs.

suzanne and sally, who were born on tuesday, april 1, are only three weeks old. since their mother would not raise them, the cubs joined the other babies in the zoo nursery. mr. joseph r. bars who enjoys raising them himself, said, "these cubs make me feel like a grandfather, since i remember raising their parents in this very nursery."

1. _____ 8. _____
2. _____ 9. _____
3. _____ 10. _____
4. _____ 11. _____
5. _____ 12. _____
6. _____ 13. _____
7. _____

1. _____ 7. _____
2. _____ 8. _____
3. _____ 9. _____
4. _____ 10. _____
5. _____ 11. _____
6. _____

★ **PART II:** Write a paragraph about Gonzo the Gorilla, who loves to watch television in his cage. Use correct capitalization in your paragraph, and include the following information:
- Who is the story about?
- Where does the story take place?
- When does the story take place?
- What shows does the gorilla enjoy watching?

Add any other information you want to make your paragraph more interesting.

The Living End — Ending Punctuation

The **PERIOD** (.) is a punctuation mark used at the end of a sentence that makes a statement, and also after initials and abbreviations.

EXAMPLES: The television show was narrated by Mr. M. A. Broadcaster in Washington, D. C. yesterday.

The **QUESTION MARK** (?) is a punctuation mark used at the end of a sentence that asks a question.

EXAMPLES: Was the movie good?
When is your favorite program on television?

The **EXCLAMATION POINT** (!) is a punctuation mark used at the end of a statement showing surprise or strong feeling.

EXAMPLES: Wow! The movie was great!
That contestant won $25,000 on my favorite TV show!

Speaking of Sports

**BE A SPORT AND HELP SOME ATHLETES AND FANS
SPEAK FOR THEMSELVES!**

★ **PART I:** Write a sentence in each cartoon balloon below, using the correct punctuation mark to end each sentence. You must use each of these marks at least once—a period (.), a question mark (?), and an exclamation point (!).

BONUS

★ **PART II:** Create your own sports cartoon. Write what each character is saying, and punctuate your sentences correctly.

Common Commas

A **COMMA** (,) is a punctuation mark used in several ways to indicate a pause in the reading of written materials. The **COMMA** aids the reader in understanding and interpreting information.

Some common uses of COMMAS are:
1. To separate words and phrases in a series.
    Example: The magazine contained articles about hobbies, crafts, games, sports, and travel.
2. To separate parts of dates and to separate names of cities from states or countries.
    Examples: Monday, December 11, 1980
            Baltimore, Maryland   Rome, Italy
3. To separate two sentences joined together by conjunctions such as "but, and, or." (separating clauses of compound sentences)
    Example: The actors performed for several hours, and the audience applauded wildly.
4. To set apart (a) introductory phrases and (b) long phrases or clauses.
    Examples: After several hours,[a] the raging storm ended suddenly,[b] so that the postponed show could continue.
5. To set off explanatory words and phrases.
    Example: Hug, a popular rock group, will perform tonight.
6. To set off a direct quotation.
    Examples: "Let's get on with the show," called the director.
            The star replied, "I'm not ready yet."

HEY, ARE YOU AS BUSY AS I AM?

, ,

YES! I HAVE TO SEPARATE WORDS IN A SERIES, SET OFF DIRECT QUOTATIONS, AND WORK OVERTIME INSIDE SENTENCES.

From *The Basics and Beyond* © 1981, Goodyear Publishing Co., Inc.

Comma Cinema

PREPARE YOURSELF FOR VIEWING A NEW SCIENCE FICTION MOVIE!

```
COMING SOON
RETURN TO GALAXY NOVA
BOLD  DARING  EXCITING
```

★ Read the movie announcement below in which commas have been omitted. Use the rules listed in the preceding "Common Commas" section to help you, and place commas where they belong in each sentence.

ADVERTISEMENT

See the all new space adventure "Return to Galaxy Nova" coming soon to neighborhood theaters. Thrill at the incredible special effects as starships clash rockets explode and planets collide! Because you've been waiting so long for this film the producers have spared no expense in bringing you a dramatic fast-paced amusing and heartwarming story. The Gazette's movie critic C. A. Film has commented "This is the space adventure of all times!"

"Return to Galaxy Nova" will premiere in Boston Massachusetts on Friday January 1. It will open at a theater near you on Saturday January 15 and it is sure to bring you hours of pleasure. If you enjoy chills and thrills don't miss it!

From *The Basics and Beyond* © 1981, Goodyear Publishing Co., Inc.

Comma Confusion

CAN COMMAS MAKE A DIFFERENCE? FIND OUT FOR YOURSELF!

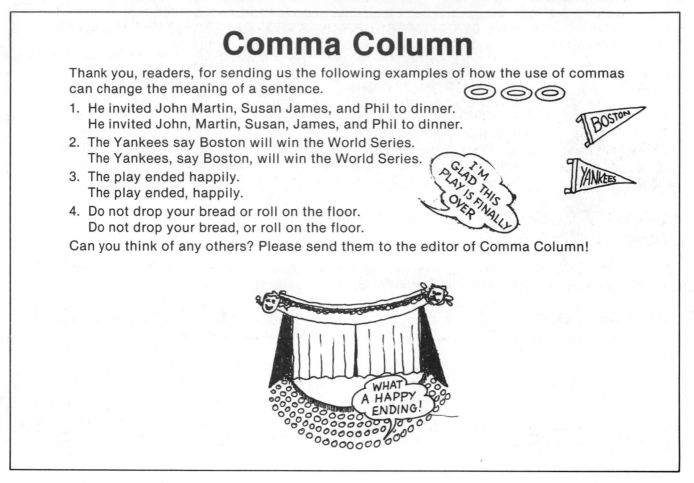

Comma Column

Thank you, readers, for sending us the following examples of how the use of commas can change the meaning of a sentence.

1. He invited John Martin, Susan James, and Phil to dinner.
   He invited John, Martin, Susan, James, and Phil to dinner.
2. The Yankees say Boston will win the World Series.
   The Yankees, say Boston, will win the World Series.
3. The play ended happily.
   The play ended, happily.
4. Do not drop your bread or roll on the floor.
   Do not drop your bread, or roll on the floor.

Can you think of any others? Please send them to the editor of Comma Column!

I'M GLAD THIS PLAY IS FINALLY OVER

WHAT A HAPPY ENDING!

★ Below are four sentences, each with an explanation of what that sentence is supposed to mean. Put commas in the appropriate places in each sentence, so that the sentence will convey the correct meaning.

1. You went with Alex Charles Jill Phillips and Greg to the movies.
   (Meaning: You went with three friends to the movies; use 2 commas.)
2. Newburg School's basketball team will play Jackson which tied Jefferson and Adams.
   (Meaning: Newburg's team will play Jackson and Adams schools in basketball. Jackson tied Jefferson in a previous game; use 2 commas.)
3. I'm coming to the party with Julie Harris.
   (Meaning: You're telling a friend named Harris that you are coming to the party with Julie; use one comma.)
4. Don't play the piano or drum with your fingers.
   (Meaning: You're asking someone not to play the piano and not to make drumming noises with his fingers; use one comma.)

From *The Basics and Beyond* © 1981, Goodyear Publishing Co., Inc.

Riddled Quotes

QUOTATION MARKS (" ") are punctuation marks used to note the exact words of a speaker. They are placed at the beginning and the end of the words being quoted. A comma is usually used to set apart the words being quoted. However, if a quote is in the form of a question or an exclamation, a question mark or exclamation point is used directly after the quote, instead of a comma.

EXAMPLES:
1. "I can't wait," stated Nate.
"Why not?" asked Dot.
"It's too late!" shouted Kate.
Clyde replied, "Come for the ride."
2. "What would you do if an elephant sat in front of you at a movie?" asked the comedian.
Someone in the audience answered, "I'd probably miss most of the movie."

BECOME A COMEDIAN AND REWRITE SOME JOKES FROM A RIDDLE BOOK!

★ **PART I:** Rewrite the following jokes by making each one contain a quotation. Punctuate each joke correctly by using quotation marks where needed.

EXAMPLES: What did one tube of glue say to the other tube of glue? (We have to stick together.)
Rewrite: "We have to stick together," said one tube of glue to the other.

In addition to using the word *said* in your sentences, add variety by using words such as *commented, explained, argued, yelled, pleaded, asked.*

1. What did the can say to the can opener?
(You make me flip my lid.)

_____

2. What did the adding machine say to the cashier?
(You can count on me.)

_____

3. What did the painter say to the wall?
(One more crack and I'll plaster you!)

_____

4. What did one dandelion say to the other dandelion?
(Take me to your weeder.)

_____

5. What did the rug say to the floor?
(Don't move, I've got you covered!)

_____

6. What did George Washington say to his men before they crossed the Delaware River?
(Get in the boat.)

_____

7. What did Paul Revere say at the end of his famous ride?
(Whoa!)

_____

8. What did one duck say to the other duck?
(You quack me up.)

_____

9. What did one light say to the other light?
(Let's go out tonight.)

_____

10. What did one wall say to the other wall?
(Let's meet at the corner.)

_____

BONUS

★ **PART II:** Make up one or two of your own jokes with quotations in them. Choose your own topic or select one from the suggestions below. Illustrate your jokes if you wish!

What did the horse say to its rider?
What did the ice cream say to the cone?
What did the football say to the kicker?
What did the tape say to the tape recorder?

_____

_____

_____

_____

_____

From *The Basics and Beyond* © 1981, Goodyear Publishing Co., Inc.

Punctuation Puns

JOIN *GROOVE* IN SOME PUN FUN!

★ **PART I:**   Each sentence below contains a pun, or a play on words, called a "Tom Swiftie." These pun sentences were named after a book character called Tom Swift, who often used special words to describe his actions.

> **EXAMPLES:**   "Watch out for that *tack,*" Tom said *sharply.* Tom noted *fruitlessly,* "I've lost all of my *apples.*"

Read the other Tom Swifties that follow, and punctuate them properly. Remember to set off direct quotes with quotation marks, to use commas where needed, and to end statements with periods. Use the example above to help you.

1. The water is fine called Tom swimmingly
2. I love chocolate Tom commented sweetly
3. Tom said heartily Happy Valentine's Day
4. Tom replied off-handedly I'll never feed a lion again
5. I'm a prince Tom remarked charmingly
6. The rain ruined our picnic Tom grumbled stormily

BONUS

★ **PART II:**   Try creating your own Tom Swifties, and remember to punctuate them properly. You might want to use some of the following words: rapidly, flatly, smoothly, magically, crisply, shockingly, icily.

1. _____
2. _____
3. _____
4. _____
5. _____

Wildlife Trivia
(Or "Everything You Never Wanted to Know About Animals")

PARENTHESES ( ) are punctuation marks used to enclose extra information or information that clarifies a statement.

EXAMPLES: The gila monster is the only poisonous lizard in the United States (although its poison does not seem to be fatal to humans).

LEARN SOME WILDLIFE TRIVIA FACTS (AND IMPRESS YOUR FRIENDS)

★ **PART I:**   Match each wildlife trivia fact* with the information in parentheses that explains or describes that fact. Place the letter of each group of words in parentheses beside the correct numbered fact.

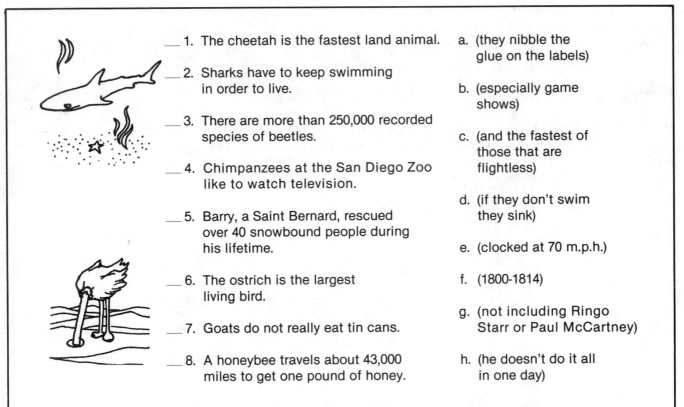

___ 1. The cheetah is the fastest land animal.

___ 2. Sharks have to keep swimming in order to live.

___ 3. There are more than 250,000 recorded species of beetles.

___ 4. Chimpanzees at the San Diego Zoo like to watch television.

___ 5. Barry, a Saint Bernard, rescued over 40 snowbound people during his lifetime.

___ 6. The ostrich is the largest living bird.

___ 7. Goats do not really eat tin cans.

___ 8. A honeybee travels about 43,000 miles to get one pound of honey.

a. (they nibble the glue on the labels)

b. (especially game shows)

c. (and the fastest of those that are flightless)

d. (if they don't swim they sink)

e. (clocked at 70 m.p.h.)

f. (1800-1814)

g. (not including Ringo Starr or Paul McCartney)

h. (he doesn't do it all in one day)

*These wildlife facts were taken from *The Joy of Trivia* by Bernie Smith (Brooke House Publishers, Chatsworth, Calif., 1976), and *The Book of Lists* by David Wallechinsky, Irving Wallace, and Amy Wallace (Bantam Books, N.Y., 1978).

From *The Basics and Beyond* © 1981, Goodyear Publishing Co., Inc.

★ **PART II:** Read the sentences below. Decide what information in each could be considered extra information. Put parentheses around the "extra information" in each sentence.*

1. All penguins live in the Southern Hemisphere; none live near the North Pole.

2. Tortoises can live to be over 100, with the oldest recorded age of a tortoise being 116.

3. The red wolf, who lives along the gulf coast of Texas, is considered to be an endangered species.

4. The koala, the wallaby, and the kangaroo, all found in Australia, raise their young in pouches.

5. Morris, the cat on television commercials for Nine-Lives Cat Food, had around-the-clock guards to protect him from kidnappers.

*These facts were taken from *The Book of Lists* by David Wallechinsky, Irving Wallace, and Amy Wallace (Bantam Books, N.Y., 1978).

Punctuation Press

THE PUNCTUATION PRESS WHEEL

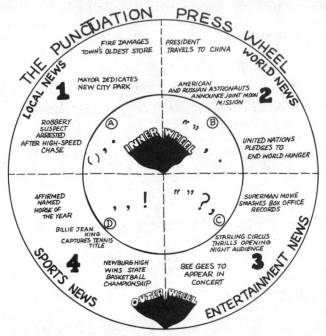

START THE PRESSES! REPORT SOME NEWS FOR A LOCAL NEWSPAPER!

★ Select any one numbered section from the Outer Wheel (local, world, entertainment, or sports news) and any one lettered section (A,B,C,D) from the Inner Wheel pictured above. Using all of the punctuation marks within the Inner Wheel section you choose, write a sentence about one of the headlines from the Outer Wheel news section you selected.

Write a total of four news sentences, each using a combination of one headline and one set of punctuation marks found on the Punctuation Press Wheel.

EXAMPLE:	Outer Wheel number / Inner Wheel letter	4/C (headline) Billie Jean King Captures Tennis Title
	(sentence) A fan asked , " Did you think you were going to win ? "	

1. ___/___ _____

_____

2. ___/___ _____

_____

3. ___/___ _____

_____

4. ___/___ _____

_____

From *The Basics and Beyond* © 1981, Goodyear Publishing Co., Inc.

Mark My Words

> A **PUNCTUATION MARK** is a written symbol used to give added clarity or expression to written material.

> Some common PUNCTUATION MARKS are the (.) period, (,) comma, (') apostrophe, (?) question mark, (!) exclamation point, (:) colon, (;) semicolon, (" ") quotation marks, (-) hyphen, and ( ) parentheses.

PUT YOURSELF IN THE PLACE OF A PUNCTUATION MARK, AND GRANT AN INTERVIEW TO THE *PUNCTUATION POST*, A GRAMMAR NEWSLETTER

★ **PART I:** Select two punctuation marks from those listed above. Write two sentences telling how it would feel to be each punctuation mark. Refer to the following student-written samples.

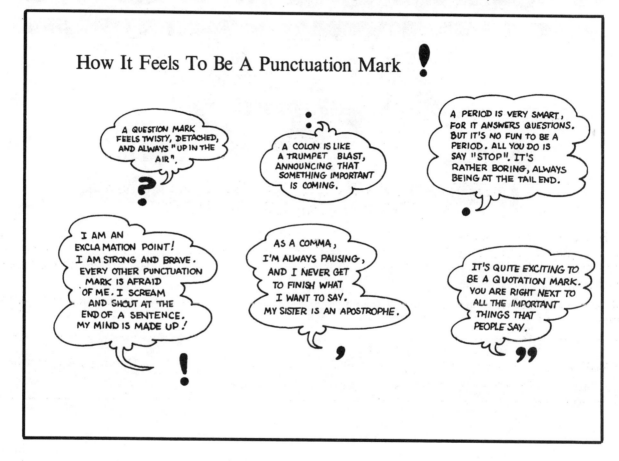

★ **PART II:** Invent a new punctuation mark. Explain how that mark would be used, and then use it in a written sentence.

EXAMPLE:	New Mark: ☺ a smile dot
	Used for: ending a happy sentence
	Sentence: It was an incredibly marvelous day ☺

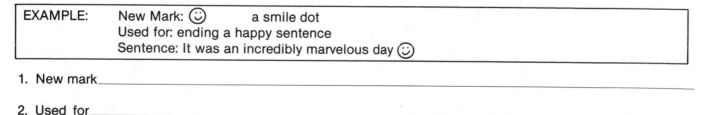

1. New mark _____

2. Used for _____

3. Sentence _____

From *The Basics and Beyond* © 1981, Goodyear Publishing Co., Inc.

2 TOMORROW
Apply Your Skills

S E C T I O N O N E

The Real World: Recording Personal Information

It's in the Schedule

A **SCHEDULE** is an organized listing of specific events or activities, noted in the order in which they occur.

SCHEDULE SOME CARNIVAL EVENTS AND PERSONAL ACTIVITIES

★ You are in charge of setting up the Special Events schedule for the annual Newburg Community Carnival. Read the information below and then write your time schedule in the form that follows. (Keep in mind that only *one* special event can be scheduled during each one half hour, and that all ten events must be scheduled during the hours of 10:00 A.M. to 3:00 P.M.)

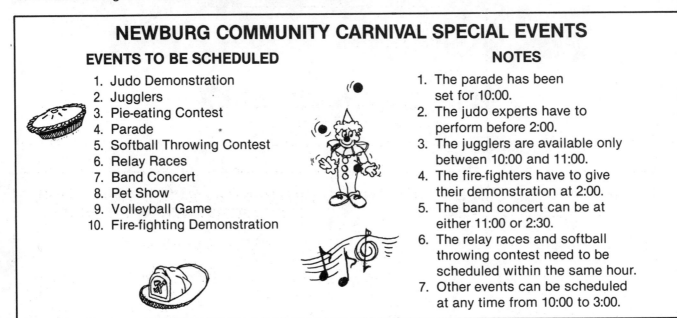

NEWBURG COMMUNITY CARNIVAL SPECIAL EVENTS

EVENTS TO BE SCHEDULED

1. Judo Demonstration
2. Jugglers
3. Pie-eating Contest
4. Parade
5. Softball Throwing Contest
6. Relay Races
7. Band Concert
8. Pet Show
9. Volleyball Game
10. Fire-fighting Demonstration

NOTES

1. The parade has been set for 10:00.
2. The judo experts have to perform before 2:00.
3. The jugglers are available only between 10:00 and 11:00.
4. The fire-fighters have to give their demonstration at 2:00.
5. The band concert can be at either 11:00 or 2:30.
6. The relay races and softball throwing contest need to be scheduled within the same hour.
7. Other events can be scheduled at any time from 10:00 to 3:00.

NEWBURG COMMUNITY CARNIVAL SCHEDULE OF SPECIAL EVENTS

10:00–10:30 _____

10:30–11:00 _____

11:00–11:30 _____

11:30–12:00 _____

12:00–12:30 _____

12:30–1:00 _____

1:00–1:30 _____

1:30–2:00 _____

2:00–2:30 _____

2:30–3:00 _____

From *The Basics and Beyond* © 1981, Goodyear Publishing Co., Inc.

Calendar Countdown

A **CALENDAR** is a table of dates organized by days, months, seasons, or years.

MAKE A DATE! BEGIN THE NEW YEAR BY PLANNING AND ORGANIZING YOUR ACTIVITIES

★ Below is a list of community activities offered in January. Organize your plans by selecting the events and classes that interest you, and by recording the names and times of those events and classes in the appropriate calendar spaces for January. Remember to record five events and two classes on your calendar.

> *ATTEND five events* of your choice at the Newburg Center
>
> *AND*
>
> *TAKE two classes* offered by the Newburg Recreation Department

JANUARY—NEWBURG CENTER SCHEDULE OF EVENTS

3-NBA Basketball Game	7 P.M.
5-Starling Circus	8 P.M.
10-Professional Wrestling	7:30 P.M.
12-NHL Hockey Game	8 P.M.
13-Ice Follies on Parade	4 P.M.
14-Boat and Camping Show	1-5 P.M.
19-Wild West Rodeo	7:30 P.M.
20-Rock Concert	7:30 P.M.
21-International Horse Show	3-8 P.M.
26-Disco Dance Competition	7 P.M.
29-Country/Western Concert	8 P.M.
30-State Gymnastic Competition	7 P.M.

NEWBURG RECREATION DEPARTMENT SCHEDULE OF JANUARY CLASSES

Classes start the week of Jan. 8 and end Jan. 27

First Aid	Fri.	4-5 P.M.
Ice Skating	Mon./Wed.	4-5 P.M.
Trampoline	Tue./Thurs.	4-5 P.M.
Clay Modeling	Sat.	10-11 A.M.
Skateboarding	Fri.	4-5 P.M.
Arts and Crafts	Mon.	4-5 P.M.
Tumbling	Sat.	9-10 A.M.
Horseback Riding	Sat.	1-3 P.M.
Bowling	Wed.	4-5 P.M.
Guitar	Mon./Wed.	7-8 P.M.
Indoor Swimming	Thurs.	7-8 P.M.

JANUARY 19

SUNDAY	MONDAY	TUESDAY	WEDNESDAY	THURSDAY	FRIDAY	SATURDAY
	1 New Year's Day	2	3	4	5	6
7	8	9	10	11	12	13
14	15	16	17	18	19	20
21	22	23	24	25	26	27
28	29	30	31			

DECEMBER

S	M	T	W	T	F	S
					1	2
3	4	5	6	7	8	9
10	11	12	13	14	15	16
17	18	19	20	21	22	23
24	25	26	27	28	29	30
31						

FEBRUARY

S	M	T	W	T	F	S
				1	2	3
4	5	6	7	8	9	10
11	12	13	14	15	16	17
18	19	20	21	22	23	24
25	26	27	28			

January

Make a List

A **LIST** is a written record of things to do, buy, or remember, and is used to help organize items, thoughts, or ideas.

ORGANIZE YOUR LIFE! MAKE SOME LISTS TO HELP YOU

★ **PART I:** You have moved into a new home and are helping unpack the boxes for your room. From the items noted below, list those that you might find in each box that you are unpacking. Place your answers in the appropriate illustrated boxes.

ITEMS

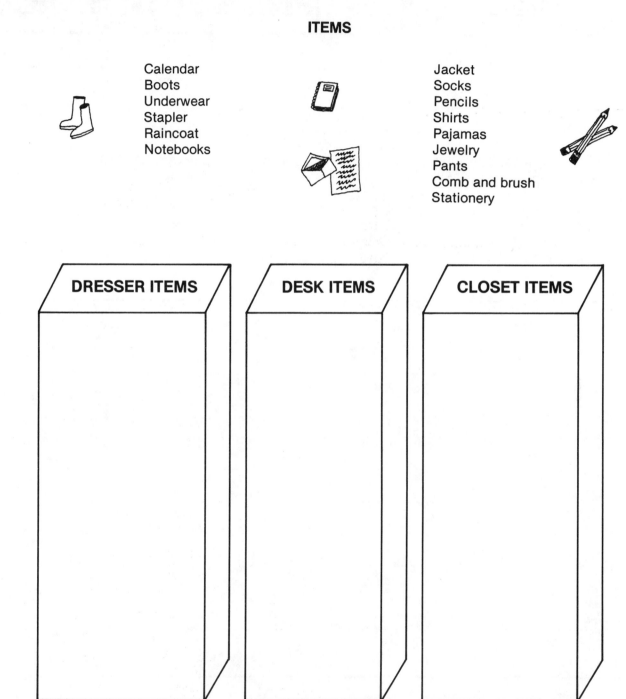

Calendar
Boots
Underwear
Stapler
Raincoat
Notebooks

Jacket
Socks
Pencils
Shirts
Pajamas
Jewelry
Pants
Comb and brush
Stationery

DRESSER ITEMS

DESK ITEMS

CLOSET ITEMS

★ **PART II:**   Your family is planning a camping trip and needs to buy several items. In each store window illustrated below, list three items that you might purchase in that store for your trip.

_____

_____

_____

★ **PART III:**   Choose one of the topics below. Make a list of ten different items you would need to buy or pack for that topic.

- taking a winter weekend skiing trip
- taking a summer weekend beach trip
- going on a picnic with three friends
- stocking a medicine cabinet
- supplying a tool kit

TOPIC: _____

1. _____

2. _____

3. _____

4. _____

5. _____

6. _____

7. _____

8. _____

9. _____

10. _____

Looking at Logs

A **LOG** is a written record of daily activities or events, stated in the order in which they occurred.

EXAMPLE:

Saturday

DAILY LOG

8:00–8:30—Woke up and ate breakfast
9:00–11:00—Mowed the lawn
11:00–12:00—Baseball practice
12:00–12:30—Lunch

HELP WRITE A LOG OF DAILY ACTIVITIES DURING AN OVERNIGHT NATURE PROGRAM

★ **PART I:** After reading the letter below describing the events of an overnight trip with the Outobon Nature Society, fill in the missing information in the log that follows. To complete the log, you will need to fill in both missing times and activities in the blank spaces.

Dear friend,   July 16

    I wanted to tell you about my terrific overnight trip with the Outobon Nature Society. We left the Outobon Society Headquarters at nine o'clock in the morning to go to our campsite, which was an hour away. When we arrived we were assigned bunks and we unpacked. At noon we got ready for lunch and raised the flag. Fifteen minutes later we were eating our bag lunches. Next, at one o'clock, we took an hour orientation hike, where we were shown the camp grounds and the facilities. Right after that we were assigned to groups, and our group took a forestry hike that lasted for two and one-half hours. We went on a trail and identified forty kinds of trees and rocks. It was really tiring, but I enjoyed it.

    At four-thirty the camp staff finally gave us free time and I played volleyball. Supper was an hour late, but fifteen minutes before supper I had K-P (kitchen patrol) duty! It wasn't really that bad. Supper lasted an hour, and after supper we lowered the flag during a fifteen-minute ceremony. At eight o'clock we saw an ecology movie, which lasted for an hour and a half. It was pretty interesting, and I learned a lot about conservation. Oh, I forgot to mention that we had an hour and fifteen minutes of free time before the movie. I played ping pong and won every game I played! It was lights out at half past nine, and I was exhausted!

    The next day we got up at seven o'clock and cleaned bunks. We had flag raising (for fifteen minutes) an hour later. Next was breakfast, and I don't think I've ever eaten so much! At nine o'clock our group left for an ecology hike, where we examined soil samples and studied small plants and pond animals. Three hours later we returned just in time for an hour-long lunch. After one hour of free time we visited a nearby farm to observe modern farming practices, and we spent two hours there. After we returned from the farm it was four o'clock, and time to lower the flag. Fifteen minutes later we left camp to return home.

    We finally arrived back at the Outobon Society Headquarters an hour later. I wrote a log of the events of my overnight trip, but I can't seem to find it. After writing this letter, though, it should be easy to rewrite my log!

Your friend,

Nat Ural

From *The Basics and Beyond* © 1981, Goodyear Publishing Co., Inc.

LOG—Outobon Nature Society Trip

Thursday, July 14
TIME   ACTIVITY

9:00 A.M. _____   _____

 –12:00 _____   _____

12:00–12:15 _____   _____

_____   lunch _____

_____   _____

4:30–5:15 _____   _____

_____   K-P duty _____

5:30–6:30 _____   _____

_____   _____

6:45–8:00 _____   free time _____

_____   movie on ecology _____

9:30 P.M. _____   _____

Friday, July 15
TIME   ACTIVITY

_____   _____

8:00–8:15 _____   _____

_____   breakfast _____

_____   _____

12:00–1:00 _____   _____

_____   free time _____

_____   _____

4:00–4:15 _____   _____

_____ P.M.   arrived at Outobon Headquarters

★ **PART II:**   Write a log recording the events of today or of another day during the current week.

DAILY LOG

Date_____   Name_____

TIME   ACTIVITY

BONUS

★ **PART III:**   Write a "feelings" log describing how you felt during each of the events noted in the log above.

Journal Journey

A **JOURNAL** is a personal written record of thoughts, ideas, feelings, ideas, and experiences.

Examples of Journal Styles: • **TRIP TO MARINELAND** •

- *EVENTS–JOURNAL OF EVENTFUL EDNA*
  (factual recording of experiences and events)

  While visiting Marineland I saw a sea mammal show, where dolphins performed tricks and played basketball. I also viewed man-eating white sharks in a huge glass tank.

- *REFLECTIONS–JOURNAL OF REFLECTIVE RON*
  (recording of personal thoughts and feelings related to an experience)

  The playful, intelligent dolphins and leering, awesome sharks at Marineland made me appreciate the variety of life that exists in our oceans. I feel that every creature has the right to exist, and that people should work to save animals from becoming extinct.

USE A JOURNAL TO RECORD SOME MEMORABLE EXPERIENCES

★ **PART I:** Choose one of the journal styles described above. Then, using the style of either Eventful Edna (or Ed) or Reflective Ron (or Rhonda), write journal entries in the Journal spaces provided about a 2-day hike in the mountains. Base your journal entries on the information listed below.

DAY #1	DAY #2
1. 5-mile hike up rugged mountain	1. awakened by raccoons knocking over trash cans
2. saw bears	2. got two bee stings
3. lost trail for one half hour	3. crossed stream on shaky log
4. ate lunch beside a waterfall	4. fell in stream
5. camped overnight in a tent	5. completed hike at sunset

Journal of Day #1

Journal of Day #2

From *The Basics and Beyond* © 1981, Goodyear Publishing Co., Inc.

★ PART II: Choose one of the topics below and write a journal entry about your (real or imaginary) experience.

- Bike Trip
- First Day at a New School
- An All-day Babysitting Job
- Training or Caring for a New Pet
- Sports Competition (swim meet, bowling tournament, team game, etc.)
- Other (topic of your choice)

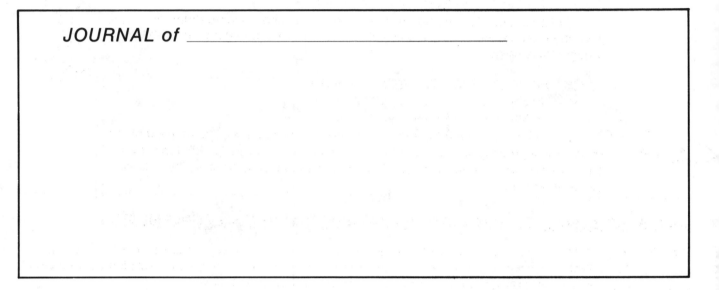

JOURNAL of _____

BONUS

★ PART III: Keep a journal of your ideas, feelings, and activities for one week. Try writing some entries in an "event" style, and some in a "reflections" style. You may want to share your journal with a teacher or a friend.

From *The Basics and Beyond* © 1981, Goodyear Publishing Co., Inc.

Resumé Review

A **RESUME'** is a summary of personal information and qualifications for a job or office.

REVIEW YOUR QUALIFICATIONS AND FILL OUT A RESUME FOR A JOB OR AN ELECTED SCHOOL OFFICE

★ Pick and apply for one job or office from the school bulletin board below. Then complete the resume form that is provided.

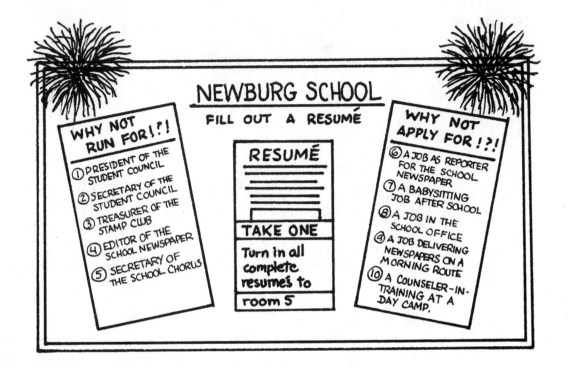

RESUMÉ

I. *PERSONAL INFORMATION*

Name_____ Date _____

Address_____ Phone _____

   _____

Date of Birth_____

Hobbies or Special Interests_____

II. *POSITION DESIRED*_____

III. *QUALIFICATIONS*

Membership in Organizations_____

Offices Held_____

Job Experience_____

   _____

Other Qualifications_____

IV. *REFERENCES*

(Names and addresses of two persons other than members of your family who can be contacted to recommend you for the job or office you are seeking)

1. _____

2. _____

- -

STATEMENT (Attach to resumé)

   Explain why you think that you are the best candidate for the office or job. Limit your response to one paragraph.

SECTION TWO

The Real World: Responding to the Demands of Society

While You Were Out

A **PHONE MESSAGE** is a written communication about a phone call which was received.

LISTEN CAREFULLY AND TAKE SOME PHONE MESSAGES

Phone Messages Should Include:

From: (Name of Caller)	Constance Talker
For: (Name of person who caller wishes to speak with)	Helen Helpful
Date	March 2
Time: (Time phone call was received)	Sat., 12:30 p.m.
Message: (Brief statement about the .... call, such as if the call is to be returned and phone number to call)	Please have Helen call back at Suzi's house. Phone No.—549-0001. Also, Helen can come over tonight at 7:30.
Message Taken By: (Name of person writing message)	Harry Helpful

HARRY HELPFUL'S HINTS:

1. Always ask who is calling and if you can take a message.

2. If you can't understand the name of the caller, have the person spell it.

3. If a phone number is left, read it back to make sure that you have written it correctly.

★ **PART I:** You have just received the following two phone messages. Read the paragraph written about the phone calls and rewrite the information in the Phone Message Forms. Remember to write only a *brief* message, but include the main ideas.

Message #1 Alex Bell of the phone company called on March 3rd at about 5:30 p.m. after I got home from ball practice. He asked if my parents were home. He called to find out if our phone was still out of order. He said that after receiving a busy signal for several hours, four persons had called to report our phone out of order. I told him that our pet monkey had gotten loose in the house and she and our dog had probably been playing with the phone, since it was now off the hook. I told him that everything was working fine now. He said that he was glad and he hung up. But, he sounded as if he didn't believe me! Your son, Sid.

From *The Basics and Beyond* © 1981, Goodyear Publishing Co., Inc.

Phone Message #1

WHILE YOU WERE OUT

From: _____

For: _____

Date & Time: _____

Message: _____

_____

_____

Message Taken By: _____

Message #2 Dear Derek,

A lady from the pet shop named Betty Barker called. You had just left to go to the store at 3:00 and missed her call by ten minutes. She called to tell you that the cute little puppy that you bought was ready to be picked up and taken home. She said to bring a leash and plenty of newspaper for your car. I can't wait until you bring the puppy home! Oh, she said to call her if you couldn't pick up the puppy by 6:00 today (Tuesday, March 5th). The phone number she left is 550-7711. I am going over to Nikki's house for the afternoon, so I wrote you this note instead of forgetting to tell you. Your sister, Alison.

Phone Message #2

WHILE YOU WERE OUT

From: _____

For: _____

Date & Time: _____

Message: _____

_____

_____

Message Taken By: _____

★ PART II

BONUS

Make up a phone message form for your family to use. Then make up your own imaginary message, using your form.

From *The Basics and Beyond* © 1981, Goodyear Publishing Co., Inc.

Memo Madness

A **MEMO** (or **MEMORANDUM**) is a brief, concise message used to convey information or to serve as a reminder to another person or yourself.

EXAMPLE:

MEMO TO: Bea A. Student
FROM: Ima Teacher
DATE: February 1
RE: Homework
(Regarding)   Don't forget to turn in your book report by next Friday, February 8.

TAKE TIME TO "TELL IT LIKE IT IS," AND WRITE YOUR OWN MEMOS

★ **PART I:** Choose two of the topics found on the desk below. Write a memo about each topic in the memo spaces provided. The memos may be humorous or serious.

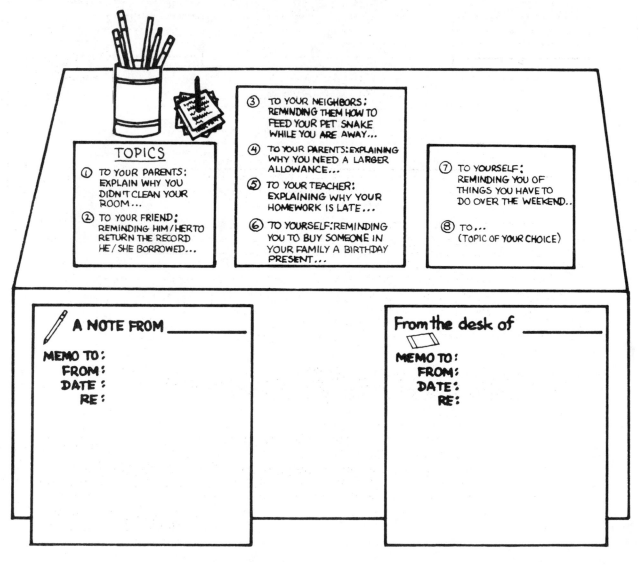

From *The Basics and Beyond* © 1981, Goodyear Publishing Co., Inc.

Post a Notice

A **NOTICE** is a brief written public announcement that gives or requests specific items of information.

WANT TO SELL, SWAP, OR ADVERTISE AN ITEM OR SERVICE? POST SOME NOTICES ON A COMMUNITY BULLETIN BOARD!

★ **PART I:** Each notice posted on the Swap Shop bulletin board was accidentally torn, and is missing necessary information. Complete each notice by finding its missing piece (shown on the table below the illustrated bulletin board) and filling in the correct information in the spaces provided on each notice.

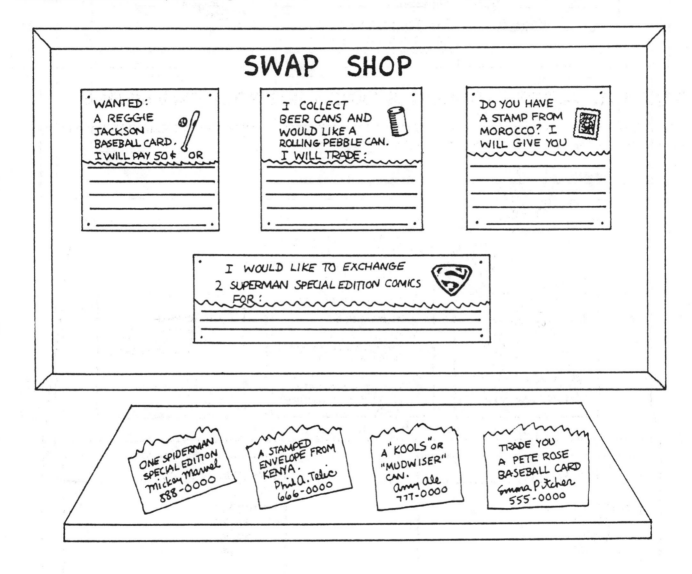

From *The Basics and Beyond* © 1981, Goodyear Publishing Co., Inc.

★ **PART II:** Write three notices for the Swap Shop bulletin board below. Choose from the listed "To Trade" items or make up some trades of your own. You may also illustrate your notices, if you wish.

SWAP SHOP

TO TRADE

1. Two *Groove* magazines for two *Scare* magazines.

2. An autograph of Andy Gibb for an autograph of _____.

3. A Washington Bullets basketball pennant for a _____ (team of your choice) pennant.

4. A Bee Gees poster for a _____ poster.

5. Two paperback mystery books for two paperback joke books.

6. Fifty *Star Wars* cards for $1.00 or fifty *Star Trek* cards.

From *The Basics and Beyond* © 1981, Goodyear Publishing Co., Inc.

★ **PART III:** Below are some examples of notices posted on the Newburg School student bulletin board. Read the examples, then write "Wanted," "For Sale," and "Services" notices of your own in the spaces provided on the board.

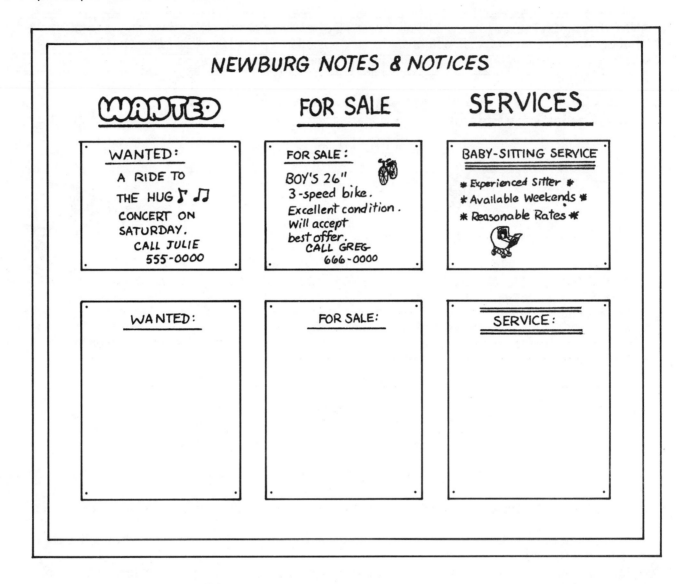

NEWBURG NOTES & NOTICES

WANTED

WANTED:
A RIDE TO
THE HUG ♪ ♫
CONCERT ON
SATURDAY.
CALL JULIE
555-0000

WANTED:

FOR SALE

FOR SALE:
BOY'S 26"
3-speed bike.
Excellent condition.
Will accept
best offer.
CALL GREG
666-0000

FOR SALE:

SERVICES

BABY-SITTING SERVICE
* Experienced Sitter *
* Available Weekends *
* Reasonable Rates *

SERVICE:

The Main Events

An **ANNOUNCEMENT** is a written public notice telling of an event or activity, or providing general information. Announcements and posters are usually posted in a public place. A **POSTER** is an illustrated announcement, briefly stating only the most important information.

CREATE YOUR OWN ANNOUNCEMENTS AND POSTERS FOR UPCOMING EVENTS

EXAMPLE OF ANNOUNCEMENT:

International Folk Dancing
Tuesday, June 5
7:00 P.M.
State School Gym

Would you like to learn to do an Armenian or Yugoslavian folk dance? How about dances from Brazil, Japan, and Denmark? Perhaps you would be interested in watching dancers, in costume, perform Hungarian or Russian Folk dances. Sound exciting? Then come join us for an evening of international folk dancing. This program is sponsored by the International Club and the Student Government.

Refreshments, which will consist of international foods, will be served and the French Club will be selling pastries.

Come and wear an international costume of your choice. Hope to see you there!

★ **PART I:** Create your own announcement by choosing one of the contests or events below. Make up and write an announcement including all of the necessary information (date, place, time, how and where to enter, etc.). Try to make the event or contest sound interesting. Also make up a poster for your topic.

TOPICS:

1. A "Write On" Contest—Raise Money for class field trips by selling stationery. The winning class goes on the first area field trip.
2. An "Art Fair"—Come and see a display of students' art work. Also, there will be centers where people can participate in art projects.
3. "Run For Your Money" Contest—Jog to raise money for the National Givers Fund Charity Drive. People pledge money for the amount of miles a student will jog.

BONUS

★ **PART II:** Make up your own announcement and poster for an event in your school or community.

From *The Basics and Beyond* © 1981, Goodyear Publishing Co., Inc.

You're Invited!

An **INVITATION** is a written or oral request for someone to attend a specific function or activity. A written invitation should include information about the activity that answers the questions: What, Who, When, Where, and Why. Special items of information may also be necessary.

TIME IS RUNNING OUT! SEND YOUR INVITATIONS EARLY

★ **PART I:** Look at the sample invitation that follows. Design and write an invitation, using one of the sets of information below.

WHAT — It's A Bowling PARTY — STRIKE UP SOME FUN!

GIVEN BY: Beth — WHO
DATE: Saturday, June 30 — WHEN
TIME: 1:00 to 4:00 p.m.
PLACE: Bowlerama — WHERE
100 Penny Lane
FOR: Beth's Birthday — WHY
R.S.V.P.: Regrets only — SPECIAL INFORMATION
301-0000

1. Your school invites your parents to a Back-to-School Night PTA meeting to meet the school staff. The meeting is on Tuesday, October 1, at 7:30 p.m. at your school. Your parents are requested to respond (RSVP), whether or not they will attend, by calling the school office at 555-1000.

2. The Record Rack store invites its customers to a special sale of all record albums in honor of the Grand Opening of a new branch store. The sale is Saturday, November 12, from noon to 6:00 at the Newburg Mall Shopping Center (107 Customer Lane). Anyone who brings the invitation will receive a free poster.

3. Senator Phil A. Buster invites local citizens to meet him at a campaign reception. The event is being held on the lawn of the Newburg Recreation Center (2700 Community Boulevard) on Sunday, August 22, from 11 a.m. to 2 p.m. There will be free games, and a picnic lunch will be provided. Informal clothes should be worn. In case of rain, the reception will be held the following Sunday (August 29) at the same time.

You Are Invited

WHAT: _____
WHO: _____
WHEN: _____
WHERE: _____
WHY: _____
SPECIAL NOTE: _____

★ **PART II:** Choose one of the occasions described below. Design and write an appropriate invitation for that occasion. Remember to include all necessary information. You will need to make up your own dates, times, names, and addresses.

- You are being honored at a special ceremony by the Red Cross for saving a friend from drowning. Invite an out-of-town relative to the ceremony.
- You are a finalist in the statewide science fair. Invite your friends to the fair.
- You are competing in a championship athletic event (tennis match; horse show; basketball, baseball, or football game; track and field competition). Invite some friends to watch you compete.
- Your uncle is working on the staff for the President of the United States. You receive an invitation to the White House for a formal dinner.
- You are planning a surprise birthday party for a friend. Invite some friends to the party.

ILLUSTRATION   INFORMATION

GIVEN BY _____

FOR _____

TIME _____

PLACE _____

DATE _____

_____

★ **PART III:**

   A. Read the guidelines and examples below to help you write a response to an invitation.

A **RESPONSE** to an invitation may be either oral or written. A written response should follow these *guidelines:*

   1. Use complete sentences.
   2. Summarize the details of the invitation (mention *where, what, when, who*).
   3. If you don't accept the invitation, explain *why*.

EXAMPLE: INVITATION	RESPONSE

It's A Bowling PARTY

STRIKE UP SOME FUN!

GIVEN BY: _Beth_
DATE: _Saturday, June 30_
TIME: _1:00 to 4:00 p.m._
PLACE: _Bowlerama_
100 Penny Lane
FOR: _Beth's Birthday_

. June 25

Dear Beth,
      I'm sorry that I can't come to your bowling party at Bowlarama on June 30th. I broke my ankle skateboarding and have to stay off my feet. Happy Birthday! Have a good time at your party.
            Best Wishes, Kevin

B. Choose any of the invitations from Parts I, II, or III of this activity. Write a response either accepting or declining (refusing) the invitation. Use the guidelines above in writing your response.

RESPONSE

_____ Date

Dear _____,

_____ Signature

Note This

A **NOTE** is a brief informal message which may be used to convey such things as thanks, congratulations, or a statement about something.

WRITE NOTES TO CONGRATULATE OR THANK A FRIEND

EXAMPLE OF THANK-YOU NOTE

(To Fred Funds, Treasurer, from Larry Leader, President of the Student Government)

Dear Fred, (Other openings: "Hi," "Hello," or other informal words)
    Thanks for your help this year as Treasurer. I really needed an expert to help rearrange our records! Well, let the next President worry!

 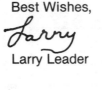

Best Wishes,

Larry

Larry Leader

(Other Closings:)

Love,
Yours,
Yours Truly,
Sincerely,
Fondly,
Gratefully,
Regards, etc.

EXAMPLE OF CONGRATULATIONS

(To Bud Brag, who just won the "Least Likely to Succeed" award, from Paul Promising)

Dear Bud,
    I know that you've always wanted to win a special award at school and now you've done it! Congratulations! Years from now we will both look back and laugh from our offices in a tall skyscraper. Of course, I may be the boss and you the employee, but we might still be able to have lunch together, sometime!

As Ever,

Paul

Paul Promising

★ Write one thank-you note and one note of congratulations in the spaces provided. You may choose one of the suggested topics below, make up your own situation, or use a real situation.

From *The Basics and Beyond* © 1981, Goodyear Publishing Co., Inc.

TOPICS FOR THANK-YOU NOTES: (Choose or make up one)

1. From the coach to the team which just lost its tenth straight game.
2. To a friend who gave you a record for your birthday. Now you have three copies.

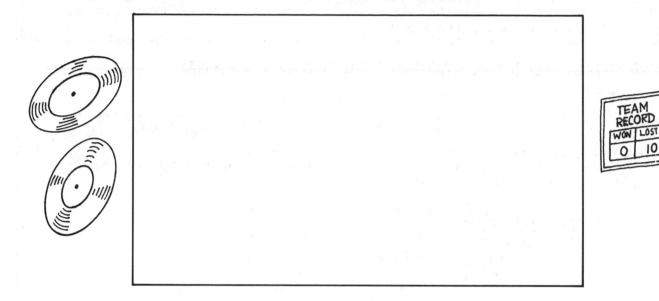

TOPICS FOR CONGRATULATIONS: (Choose or make up one)

1. To a friend who was just written up in the "You-Better-Believe-It-Or-Else-Book of World Records" for chewing one piece of bubble gum for 300 hours straight.
2. To a friend who was just selected as the fifth string relief pitcher for the school's last baseball game of the year.

From *The Basics and Beyond* © 1981, Goodyear Publishing Co., Inc.

Greetings!

GREETING CARDS convey messages noting occasions such as birthdays, holidays, and special events. They also express feelings of friendship or other personal messages.

BECAUSE YOU CARE ENOUGH TO SEND THE VERY BEST—CREATE YOUR OWN GREETING CARDS!

★ **PART I:** There are many different types of greeting cards—humorous, serious, formal, and informal. For each of the cards illustrated below, write an appropriate greeting card message for a friend. Make your message match the mood of the illustration.

★ **PART II:** Select two of the occasions noted below and create an appropriate greeting card message or poem in the spaces provided. You may add your own illustrations, if you wish.

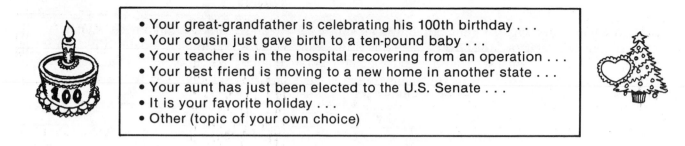

- Your great-grandfather is celebrating his 100th birthday . . .
- Your cousin just gave birth to a ten-pound baby . . .
- Your teacher is in the hospital recovering from an operation . . .
- Your best friend is moving to a new home in another state . . .
- Your aunt has just been elected to the U.S. Senate . . .
- It is your favorite holiday . . .
- Other (topic of your own choice)

Greeting Cards

From *The Basics and Beyond* © 1981, Goodyear Publishing Co., Inc.

Telegram Topics

A **TELEGRAM** is a brief message transmitted by a telegraph service and guaranteed to arrive within a few hours after being sent. (A **MAILGRAM** is a form of telegram that arrives the following day after being sent, and is less expensive to send than a regular telegram.) Since the cost of sending a telegram is based on the number of words used, messages generally include the fewest possible words. Note: It is not necessary to use complete sentences in telegram messages.

EXAMPLE:

Cousin Family
123 Main Street
Newburg

    Will arrive at bus station 2:05 PM.
    Meet me at baggage counter.
        Aunt Shellie

From *The Basics and Beyond* © 1981, Goodyear Publishing Co., Inc.

A **PUBLIC OPINION MESSAGE** is a special type of telegram, limited to fifteen words or less, that can be sent to public officials. All Public Opinion Messages cost the same amount to send, and are less expensive than regular telegrams or mailgrams.

EXAMPLE:

Senator Cool
U.S. Senate
Washington, D.C.
  Support bill SB-345 to limit hunting of
whales. Action needed to save wildlife.
      Friends of Animals Club
      Newburg School

IN A HURRY TO RELATE AN IMPORTANT MESSAGE?
SEND A TELEGRAM!

★ **PART I:** Choose two of the following personal situations and write a telegram message for each one. Use the pictured telegram forms. Make up the address to which you would be sending each telegram.

1. Aunt Matilda just won $20,000 and 5,000 oranges on the TV game show, "The Price Is Ripe." You want to congratulate her. Send a telegram.
2. You are supposed to be visiting an out-of-town friend for the weekend, but you're sick and can't go. Your friend has no telephone. Send a telegram.
3. Your school team is away preparing for a championship basketball game. You want to wish the players luck before the game. Send a telegram.
4. Your cousin was just rescued after being "lost at sea" in a boating accident. Send a telegram.

Telegram

MSG. NO	NO. WDS. CL. OF SVC.	PD.—COLL.	CASH NO.	ACCOUNTING INFORMATION	DATE	FILING TIME	SENT TIME
						A.M. P.M.	A.M. P.M.

western union

Send the following message, subject to the terms on back hereof, which are hereby agreed to.

☐ OVERNIGHT TELEGRAM UNLESS BOX ABOVE IS CHECKED THIS MESSAGE WILL BE SENT AS A TELEGRAM

CARE OF OR APT. NO.

TO

ADDRESS & TELEPHONE NO.

CITY — STATE & ZIP CODE

SENDER'S TEL. NO.   NAME & ADDRESS

Telegram

MSG. NO	NO. WDS. CL. OF SVC.	PD.—COLL.	CASH NO.	ACCOUNTING INFORMATION	DATE	FILING TIME	SENT TIME
						A.M. P.M.	A.M. P.M.

western union

Send the following message, subject to the terms on back hereof, which are hereby agreed to.

☐ OVERNIGHT TELEGRAM UNLESS BOX ABOVE IS CHECKED THIS MESSAGE WILL BE SENT AS A TELEGRAM

CARE OF OR APT. NO.

TO

ADDRESS & TELEPHONE NO.

CITY — STATE & ZIP CODE

SENDER'S TEL. NO.   NAME & ADDRESS

★ **PART II:** The Newburg Town Council is preparing to vote on a proposal on whether or not to allow construction of a large theme amusement park in the town. Write a Public Opinion Message to the Council that presents the view of any one of the following groups. (Remember, your message must be fifteen words or less.)

1. Citizens for a Clean Environment

   Position: *against* construction of the park because it might cause unnecessary pollution

2. Amusements, Inc. (the builders of the proposed park)

   Position: *in favor of* locating the park in Newburg

3. Student Government of Newburg School

   Position: _____?_____ (You decide!)

PUBLIC OPINION MESSAGE

Newburg Town Council:

_____

_____

_____

(Name of Group)

From *The Basics and Beyond* © 1981, Goodyear Publishing Co., Inc.

Postcard Practice

A **POSTCARD** is a piece of postboard used for sending short informal written messges through the mail. It does not require an envelope for mailing.
A **PICTURE POSTCARD** has an illustration or photograph on one side of the card, and requires the sender to add a stamp.
A **POST OFFICE POSTCARD** has no illustrations and is already stamped.

EXAMPLE: PICTURE POSTCARD

SAND AND SURF
AT OCEAN CITY

Dear Julie & Greg,
 We went ocean fishing yesterday. The weather's been great and I have a terrific tan!
 See you soon,
  Beth

PLACE STAMP HERE

Greg & Julie Homes
123 Main Street
Newburg ———

ILLUSTRATION

MESSAGE

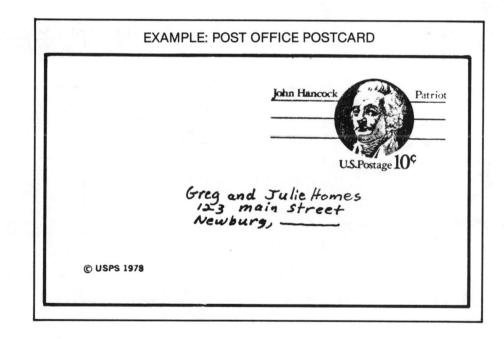

EXAMPLE: POST OFFICE POSTCARD

John Hancock Patriot

U.S. Postage 10¢

Greg and Julie Homes
123 main street
Newburg, ———

© USPS 1978

BE BRIEF! SEND YOUR MESSAGE ON A POSTCARD

★ **PART I:** Choose two of the picture postcards shown below. Imagine that you are visiting the place pictured on the postcard, and write a message briefly describing your experience. Use the postcard forms provided to address and write your messages.

WASHINGTON MONUMENT
WASHINGTON, D.C.

PLACE STAMP HERE

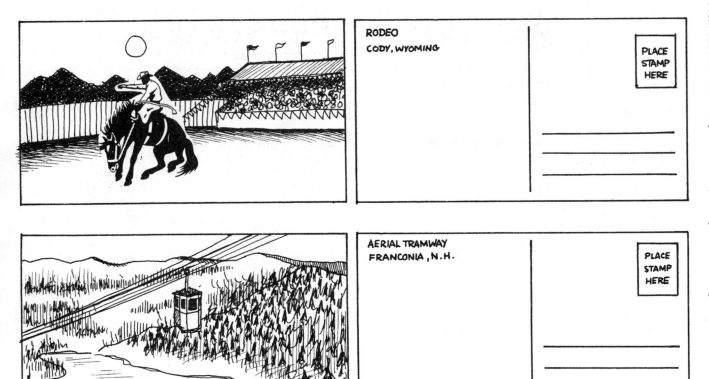

RODEO
CODY, WYOMING

PLACE STAMP HERE

AERIAL TRAMWAY
FRANCONIA, N.H.

PLACE STAMP HERE

★ **PART II:** Illustrate your own picture postcard. Write an appropriate message in the space provided.

(ILLUSTRATION)   (MESSAGE & ADDRESS)

★ **PART III:** Enter the Vacation Sweepstakes Contest described below by filling out the postcard form that follows.

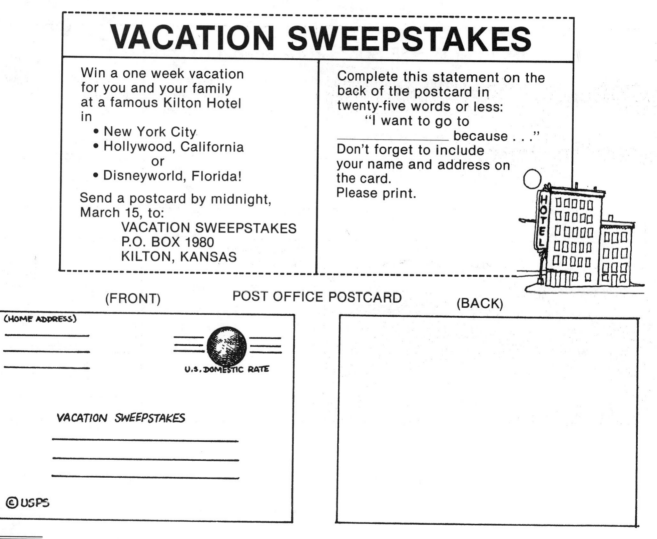

VACATION SWEEPSTAKES

Win a one week vacation for you and your family at a famous Kilton Hotel in
- New York City
- Hollywood, California
  or
- Disneyworld, Florida!

Send a postcard by midnight, March 15, to:
VACATION SWEEPSTAKES
P.O. BOX 1980
KILTON, KANSAS

Complete this statement on the back of the postcard in twenty-five words or less:
"I want to go to
_____ because . . ."
Don't forget to include your name and address on the card.
Please print.

(FRONT)   POST OFFICE POSTCARD   (BACK)

(HOME ADDRESS)

U.S. DOMESTIC RATE

VACATION SWEEPSTAKES

©USPS

BONUS

★ **PART IV:** Buy a picture postcard showing a scene from your city or state. Write a message on the back and mail it to a friend or relative who lives in another city, state, or country.

Personally Speaking

A **PERSONAL LETTER** is an informal written communication from one person to another person or group of people.

SAMPLE:

January 1, 19_____
(Date)

Dear Mom and Dad, (Greeting)

    Happy New Year! I'm really enjoying my skiing trip with Uncle Al. Don't get upset when you see the cast on my foot and the sling on my arm. I slipped on the way to the first aid station for treatment of my frostbite, but I only broke one of the new skis you gave me for my birthday.

    See you soon!

Love, (Closing)

Tracy (Signature)

EXPRESS YOURSELF! WRITE SOME PERSONAL LETTERS

★ **PART I:** Imagine that you are Noah Tall, the writer of an advice column for a newspaper. You have just received the following requests for advice from several well-known people. After reading the example below, write informal letters in response to any two of the letters that follow. Write your responses on the pictured stationery. Your responses may be serious or humorous.

FEBRUARY 22

DEAR NOAH,
    I JUST RECEIVED A NEW HATCHET FOR MY BIRTHDAY, AND USED IT TO CHOP DOWN MY DAD'S FAVORITE CHERRY TREE. SHOULD I TELL HIM I DID IT?

    PLEASE HELP ME!

    SINCERELY,

George Washington

FEBRUARY 25

DEAR GEORGE,
    YOU SHOULD TELL YOUR DAD THAT YOU'LL PAY FOR HIS TREE WITH YOUR OWN MONEY. REALLY IMPRESS HIM BY DRAWING A PICTURE OF YOURSELF ON THE MONEY YOU USE.

    GOOD LUCK,
    Noah Tall

From *The Basics and Beyond* © 1981, Goodyear Publishing Co., Inc.

Dear Noah,
    I am being annoyed by a character named Columbus who keeps asking me for money to pay for an ocean trip to the Far East. He thinks he can get there by sailing west, but I think he might be crazy. Should I help him?

Royally yours,
Queen Isabella

Dear Noah,
    I have composed music all my life, and people have said how much they enjoy my music. Recently I have begun to lose my hearing. How can a person with a hearing loss be a composer? Should I give up my musical career? Please advise me what to do.

Harmoniously,
Ludwig von Beethoven

Dear Noah,
    I am an artist and am starting my own company to make cartoons. I am looking for a character to be the hero of my feature film. I'd like to use a mouse, but many people don't seem to like mice. Should I take a chance with the mouse, or use a giraffe instead?

Artistically,
Walt Disney

Dear Noah,
    Ever since I was a young boy I've had trouble in school. I recently took a test to become a teacher, but failed the exam. I've been thinking about writing a book about atomic energy, but I'm not sure that people will accept my ideas. What should I do?

Scientifically,
Albert Einstein

BEST ADVICE

_____ (DATE)

DEAR _____ ,

_____ ,
Noah Tall

BEST ADVICE

_____ (DATE)

DEAR _____ ,

_____ ,
Noah Tall

From *The Basics and Beyond* © 1981, Goodyear Publishing Co., Inc.

★ PART II: "Pen Pals" are people from different cities or countries who have never met, but who exchange letters to learn more about each other. Read the sample letter below from a pen pal. Then write a letter of response to that pen pal, telling something about yourself, your background, and your interests.

15th of April, 198___

Dear Pen Pal,

    I live in Gan Eden, a small communal farm, or kibbutz, near the Sea of Galilee in Israel. I go to school and also work every day in the fields, where I pick grapes and melons. I eat breakfast and lunch with the other children on the kibbutz, but spend dinnertime with my parents in our own small house.

    My hobbies are collecting stamps and playing football (you call it soccer), and I plan to become an airline pilot. Please write and tell me something about yourself.

Shalom,

Ari Handelsman

From *The Basics and Beyond* © 1981, Goodyear Publishing Co., Inc.

_____

Dear Ari,

_____
_____,

BONUS

★ **PART III:** Write to one of the following addresses and request the name of a pen pal (Note: Refer to the next activity, "Minding Your Own Business" for a sample business letter format to follow in writing your letter of request.) Begin a correspondence with the person whose name you receive.

International Friendship League
40 Mount Vernon Street
Beacon Hill
Boston, Massachusetts 02108

Student Letter Exchange
WASECA, Minnesota 56093

International Youth Service
PB 125, SF-20101
Turku 10, Finland

Dear Pen Pal
Big Blue Marble
P.O. Box 4054
Santa Barbara, California 93103

From *The Basics and Beyond* © 1981, Goodyear Publishing Co., Inc.

Minding Your Own Business

A **BUSINESS LETTER** is a formal correspondence that concerns such things as informing, requesting, inquiring, ordering, or responding to other formal letters.

The "Set Up"—Sample Format of a Business Letter

①SENDER'S ADDRESS 1721 First Street

Newburg, _____ _____
          (state) (ZIP)

②DATE January 1, _____
             (year)

Ms. Alberta Success   ③MAILING ADDRESS
The Try Harder Company
3333 Victory Court
Achievement, Ohio _____
         (ZIP code)

Dear Ms. Success:④GREETING(Dear [name or title]: To Whom It May Concern

    I would like to enroll in your course, "How to Build Self-confidence Without Even Trying." Please send me your brochure and application. Also, please inform me of the dates when the course will be offered in my area.

    Thank you for your cooperation. I look forward to hearing from you.

⑥CLOSING   Yours truly,
(Sincerely   ⑦SIGNATURE
yours; Yours
truly)   Student, Newburg School

The "Cover Up"—Sample Format of an Envelope

Jackie Complex   ①SENDER'S ADDRESS
1721 First Street
Newburg, _____ _____
      (state) (ZIP code)

Ms. Alberta Success ②MAILING
The Try Harder Company   ADDRESS
3333 Victory Court
Achievement, Ohio _____
        (ZIP code)

Consumer Complaint

BECOME AN INVOLVED CONSUMER AND WRITE LETTERS OF COMPLAINT ABOUT SOME DEFECTIVE PRODUCTS

★ **PART I:**

A. Using the information below, complete the letter of complaint to the Goodenuff Products Company. Include all four points of complaint (noted on the game box) in your letter, and tell the company what action you want them to take to satisfy your concerns. Also, fill out the sample envelope with the correct mailing information.

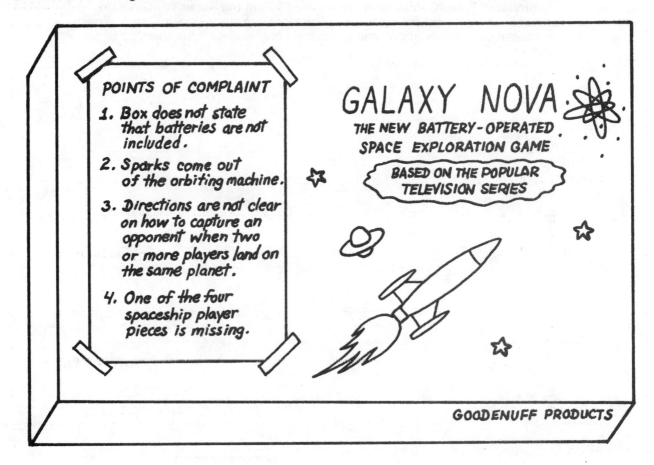

POINTS OF COMPLAINT

1. Box does not state that batteries are not included.
2. Sparks come out of the orbiting machine.
3. Directions are not clear on how to capture an opponent when two or more players land on the same planet.
4. One of the four spaceship player pieces is missing.

GALAXY NOVA
THE NEW BATTERY-OPERATED SPACE EXPLORATION GAME

BASED ON THE POPULAR TELEVISION SERIES

GOODENUFF PRODUCTS

(your address) _____

_____

Goodenuff Products
Toy Division   (date) _____
123 Main Street
Newburg, _____ 70054
                (state)

To Whom It May Concern:
    I purchased your "Galaxy Nova" game for $3.95 at the Super Toy Store on December 5, as a present for my brother. The store has since gone out of business. I have several complaints about your company's game, and I hope that you can help me.

_____

_____

_____

_____

_____

_____

_____

_____

_____

_____

                                Yours truly,

                            _____
                              (your signature)

_____ (your
address)
                            (design your
own stamp)

              _____
              _____ (company's
              _____ address)

B. Using the form provided, write a letter of response from Goodenuff Products to yourself in which they either: (1) state how they will correct your consumer problem, or (2) do not propose any action to correct your problem.

GEP

GOODENUFF PRODUCTS
"If it's not great, it's not GOODENUFF!"

Mr. Reed A. Complaint
Manager, Toy Division
Goodenuff Products
123 Main Street
Newburg, _____

Your Name _____

Your Address _____

_____

Dear_____ (Your Name):

_____

_____

_____

_____

_____

_____

_____

Yours Truly,

Reed A. Complaint

Manager, Toy Division

★ **PART II:** Described below are ten imaginary defective products. Choose one listed product or make up your own product. Using your own paper, write one *sample* letter of complaint to the imaginary Committee for More Informed Consumers, Washington D.C., 20207, stating either the safety problems of the product, any misleading consumer information, or the product's defects.

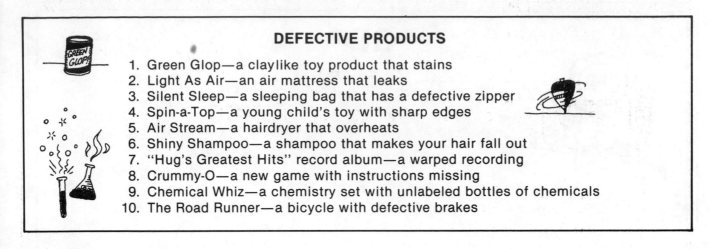

DEFECTIVE PRODUCTS

1. Green Glop—a claylike toy product that stains
2. Light As Air—an air mattress that leaks
3. Silent Sleep—a sleeping bag that has a defective zipper
4. Spin-a-Top—a young child's toy with sharp edges
5. Air Stream—a hairdryer that overheats
6. Shiny Shampoo—a shampoo that makes your hair fall out
7. "Hug's Greatest Hits" record album—a warped recording
8. Crummy-O—a new game with instructions missing
9. Chemical Whiz—a chemistry set with unlabeled bottles of chemicals
10. The Road Runner—a bicycle with defective brakes

BONUS

★ **PART III:** Choose a real product that you think is defective or unsafe and write a letter to one of the following consumer groups or organizations. Use your own stationery. Remember to proofread your letter before you mail it.

U.S. Consumer Products Safety Commission
Washington, D.C. 20207

Ralph Nader's Public Citizen
P.O. Box 19404
Washington, D.C. 20036

Consumer Reports
P.O. Box 1111
Mount Vernon, N.Y. 10550

From *The Basics and Beyond* © 1981, Goodyear Publishing Co., Inc.

Critic's Choice

BE A CRITIC! WRITE YOUR OPINION OF TELEVISION PROGRAMMING

★ **PART I:** Select one of your favorite (or least favorite) television programs. Complete the TV Review Guidelines form below to help you decide what you like (or dislike) about that program.

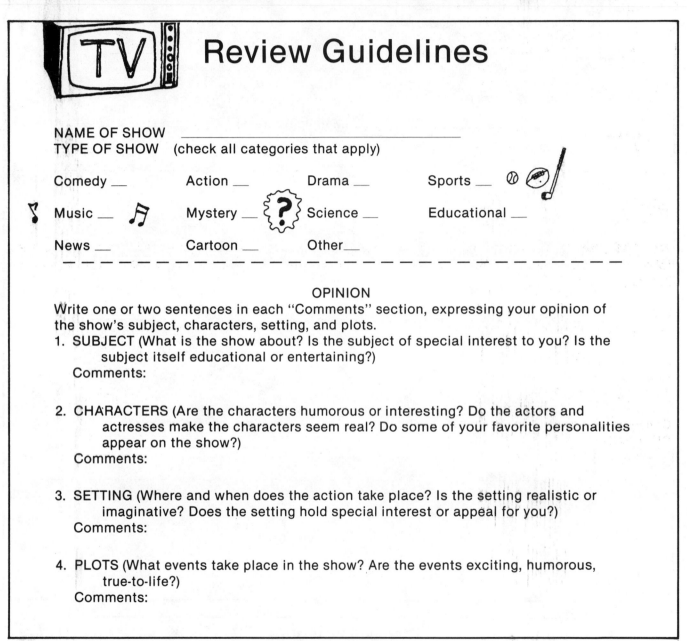

Review Guidelines

NAME OF SHOW _____

TYPE OF SHOW (check all categories that apply)

Comedy __   Action __   Drama __   Sports __

Music __   Mystery __   Science __   Educational __

News __   Cartoon __   Other __

- -

OPINION

Write one or two sentences in each "Comments" section, expressing your opinion of the show's subject, characters, setting, and plots.

1. SUBJECT (What is the show about? Is the subject of special interest to you? Is the subject itself educational or entertaining?)
   Comments:

2. CHARACTERS (Are the characters humorous or interesting? Do the actors and actresses make the characters seem real? Do some of your favorite personalities appear on the show?)
   Comments:

3. SETTING (Where and when does the action take place? Is the setting realistic or imaginative? Does the setting hold special interest or appeal for you?)
   Comments:

4. PLOTS (What events take place in the show? Are the events exciting, humorous, true-to-life?)
   Comments:

From *The Basics and Beyond* © 1981, Goodyear Publishing Co., Inc.

Write a short letter on the form provided to the producer of the show you chose, telling why you like or dislike the program. You may use the list of "TV Review Words" following the letter to help you with your writing. (Note: The actual mailing addresses of the television networks are listed in Part II of this activity.)

_____(Date)

_____(Your Address)

_____

Producer of_____

_____

_____ (Mailing Address)

_____

Dear Producer:

I am writing to express my opinion about your program, _____.

_____

_____

_____

_____

_____

_____

_____

_____

Yours truly,

_____

(Signature)

TV REVIEW WORDS
(some adjectives for television critics)

impressive	dull	senseless	meaningful	realistic
phony	dramatic	hilarious	boring	fast-paced
expressive	emotional	moving	clear	silly
frightening	insulting	clever	deadly	slow
ridiculous	incredible	suspenseful	action-packed	sad
imaginative	comical	dreadful	depressing	factual

From *The Basics and Beyond* © 1981, Goodyear Publishing Co., Inc.

BONUS

★ **PART II:** Rewrite your letter from PART I on regular stationery, or write another letter expressing your opinion about a television program or commercial. Mail your letter to the appropriate address below.

Audience Services
CBS-TV
51 West 52nd Street
New York, New York 10019

Viewer Mail
PBS (Public Broadcasting)
475 L'Enfant Plaza West, S.W.
Washington, D.C. 20024

Audience Information
ABC-TV
1330 Avenue of the Americas
New York, New York 10019

Audience Services
NBC-TV
30 Rockefeller Plaza
New York, New York 10020

Federal Trade Commission (for complaints about commercials)
Pennsylvania Avenue at Sixth Street, N.W.
Washington, D.C. 20580

From *The Basics and Beyond* © 1981, Goodyear Publishing Co., Inc.

Reviewing Requests

WRITE LETTERS TO FIND OUT WHAT YOU WANT TO KNOW

★ **PART I:** Your family is planning a trip to Washington, D.C. You had written a letter to the National Visitor Center in Washington to request information about the city, and have just received the letter below answering your questions. After reading the *letter from the Visitor Center* use the form provided to complete the *letter of request* that you might have originally written to the Center. Include at least three questions in your letter.

LETTER FROM VISITOR CENTER

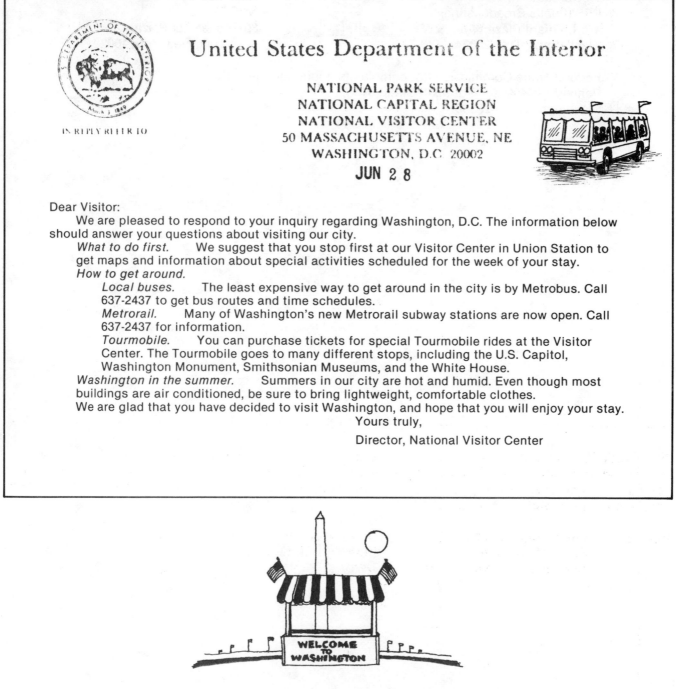

United States Department of the Interior

NATIONAL PARK SERVICE
NATIONAL CAPITAL REGION
NATIONAL VISITOR CENTER
50 MASSACHUSETTS AVENUE, NE
WASHINGTON, D.C. 20002

JUN 2 8

IN REPLY REFER TO

Dear Visitor:

We are pleased to respond to your inquiry regarding Washington, D.C. The information below should answer your questions about visiting our city.

What to do first. We suggest that you stop first at our Visitor Center in Union Station to get maps and information about special activities scheduled for the week of your stay.

How to get around.

Local buses. The least expensive way to get around in the city is by Metrobus. Call 637-2437 to get bus routes and time schedules.

Metrorail. Many of Washington's new Metrorail subway stations are now open. Call 637-2437 for information.

Tourmobile. You can purchase tickets for special Tourmobile rides at the Visitor Center. The Tourmobile goes to many different stops, including the U.S. Capitol, Washington Monument, Smithsonian Museums, and the White House.

Washington in the summer. Summers in our city are hot and humid. Even though most buildings are air conditioned, be sure to bring lightweight, comfortable clothes.

We are glad that you have decided to visit Washington, and hope that you will enjoy your stay.

Yours truly,

Director, National Visitor Center

WELCOME TO WASHINGTON

LETTER OF REQUEST

(Date)_____

(Your Address)_____

_____

_____

Director, National Visitor Center
50 Massachusetts Avenue, N.E.
Washington, D.C. 20002

Dear Director:

   My family is planning to vacation in Washington, D.C., this summer. I would be interested in receiving some information from you about _____

_____.

   I would appreciate it if you would answer some questions I have about visiting your city. _____

_____

_____

_____

_____

_____

_____.

Thank you for your help.

Yours truly,

_____

(Signature)

★ **PART II:** Choose a state that you would like to visit. On your own paper write a brief letter requesting some information (maps, pamphlets, etc.) about that state. If you wish, mail your letter. If you can't find an exact mailing address, you can send your letter to "Department of Tourism" in the capital city of the state you have selected.

Examples: Department of Tourism   Department of Tourism
             State of Maryland   State of Colorado
             Annapolis, Maryland 21401   Denver, Colorado

★ **PART III:** Listed below are several free pamphlets for which you can send away. Choose one item. Then write and mail a letter requesting that item.

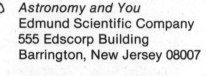

Beautiful Junk Crafts
U.S. Department of Health,
    Education, and Welfare
Office of Child Development
Washington, D.C. 20201
(Pamphlet #73-1036)

The ABCs of Knitting
Coats & Clark
P.O. Box 1010
Toccoa, Georgia 30577
(send a large self-
    addressed stamped
    envelope)

*Birds, Flowers and Trees of the
    United States; Special Report
    on Energy, Your Wildlife
    Heritage*
National Wildlife Federation
1412 16th Street, N.W.
Washington, D.C. 20036

Basketball Was Born Here
Basketball Hall of Fame
P.O. Box 175
Highland Station
460 Alden Street
Springfield, Massachusetts 01109
(send a self-addressed stamped
    envelope)

*(Almost) Everything You Wanted
    To Know About Boating . . .
    But Were Ashamed to Ask*
Outboard Boating Club of America
401 N. Michigan Ave.
Chicago, Illinois 60611

Bicycle Safety Fact Sheet
U.S. Consumer Safety Commission
Washington, D.C. 20207
Fact Sheet #10

Astronomy and You
Edmund Scientific Company
555 Edscorp Building
Barrington, New Jersey 08007

How Paper Came to America
American Paper Institute
260 Madison Avenue
New York, New York 10016

*Animal First Aid Hints; Tips on
    Feeding Your Dog or Cat*
Educational Department
American Society for the Prevention
    of Cruelty to Animals (ASPCA)
441 East 92nd Street
New York, New York 10028
(send self-addressed stamped
    envelope)

Direct Directions

DIRECTIONS are explanations of how to complete a task or activity. **WRITTEN DIRECTIONS** are used to explain such things as how to make or use a product, complete a project, master a skill, play a game, or move from one location to another. **DIRECTIONS** provide step-by-step instructions in sequential order (from the beginning step to the final step).

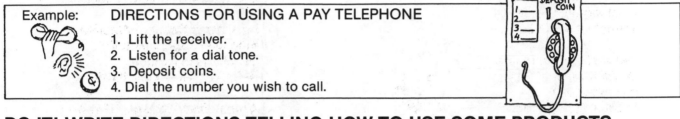

Example: DIRECTIONS FOR USING A PAY TELEPHONE

1. Lift the receiver.
2. Listen for a dial tone.
3. Deposit coins.
4. Dial the number you wish to call.

DO IT! WRITE DIRECTIONS TELLING HOW TO USE SOME PRODUCTS

★ **PART I:** Your Uncle Hermit has been living in a cave for many years and has never seen a television set before. Write directions telling him how to use the TV set pictured below to watch Killigan's Island on UHF (U) Channel 20. Use at least three steps in your directions, and list the steps in the order they should be completed.

Volume

Channel Selector

UHF Channel Selector

Color Adjustor

Step #1 ___Plug in set_____

Step #2 _____

Step #3 _____

Step #4 _____

Step #5 _____

★ PART II: Choose one of the student-designed products illustrated below. Create and write your own set of directions telling how to use that product. Give at least three, but no more than six, directions.

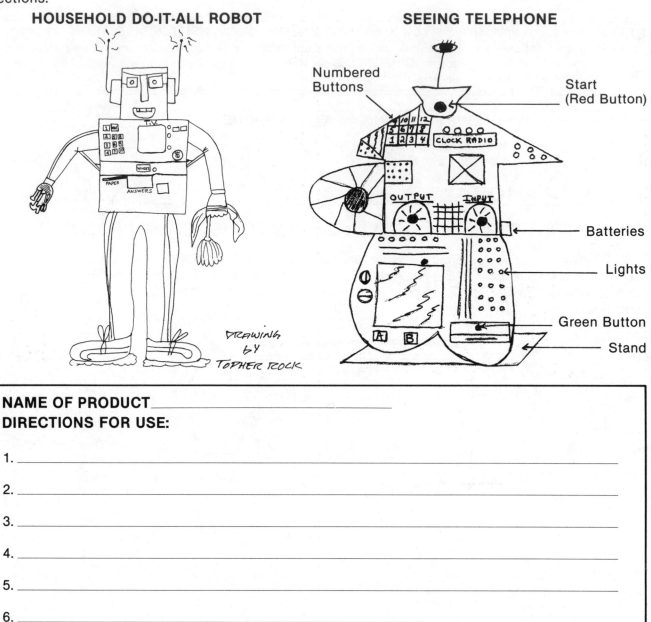

HOUSEHOLD DO-IT-ALL ROBOT

DRAWING
bY
TOPHER ROCK

SEEING TELEPHONE

Numbered Buttons

Start (Red Button)

CLOCK RADIO

OUTPUT   INPUT

Batteries

Lights

Green Button

Stand

From *The Basics and Beyond* © 1981, Goodyear Publishing Co., Inc.

NAME OF PRODUCT_____
DIRECTIONS FOR USE:

1. _____

2. _____

3. _____

4. _____

5. _____

6. _____

BONUS

★ PART III: Design a product of your own. Draw a picture of your product and write a set of directions for using it. You may choose your own type of product, or select an idea from the list below.

- vending machine
- pinball machine
- exercise machine
- homework machine
- TV of the future
- car of the future
- instant meal-maker
- computerized sports game

Easy Explanations

TRY IT! WRITE DIRECTIONS TELLING HOW TO DO SOME PHYSICAL ACTIVITIES

★ **PART I:** Look at the illustrations and written directions below for a Yoga exercise called The Rocking Horse. Then write directions explaining how to do the pictured Camel exercise.

From *The Basics and Beyond* © 1981, Goodyear Publishing Co., Inc.

Try Yoga
"ENJOYABLE EXERCISES FOR INCREASED PHYSICAL FITNESS"

The Rocking Horse

① ② ③

(1) SIT ON THE FLOOR WITH YOUR KNEES CLOSE TO YOUR CHEST AND YOUR ARMS AROUND YOUR LEGS.

(2) ROCK BACK UNTIL YOUR BACK TOUCHES THE FLOOR AND YOUR FEET ARE IN THE AIR.

(3) COME FORWARD UNTIL YOUR FEET ARE BACK ON THE FLOOR. (REPEAT SEVERAL TIMES)

The Camel

① ②

★ **PART II:** Write a set of directions for one of the following activities. Use a complete sentence for each step in your directions. If you wish, you may make illustrations for your directions.

- How to Mount a Horse
- How to Hit a Baseball
- How to Pass a Football
- How to Throw Darts
- How to Paddle a Canoe
- How to Play Freeze Tag
- How to Use a Yo-Yo
- How to Play Horseshoes
- How to Tie Your Shoes
- How to Jump Rope
- Other (activity of your own choice)

HOW TO _____

From *The Basics and Beyond* © 1981, Goodyear Publishing Co., Inc.

Craft and Cooking Corner

MAKE IT! WRITE DIRECTIONS FOR HOW TO MAKE SOME CRAFT AND FOOD ITEMS

★ **PART I:** Read the sample illustrated craft directions below entitled "How To Make a Picture Puzzle." Then write a one-sentence direction under each illustration for the Bottle Craft project.

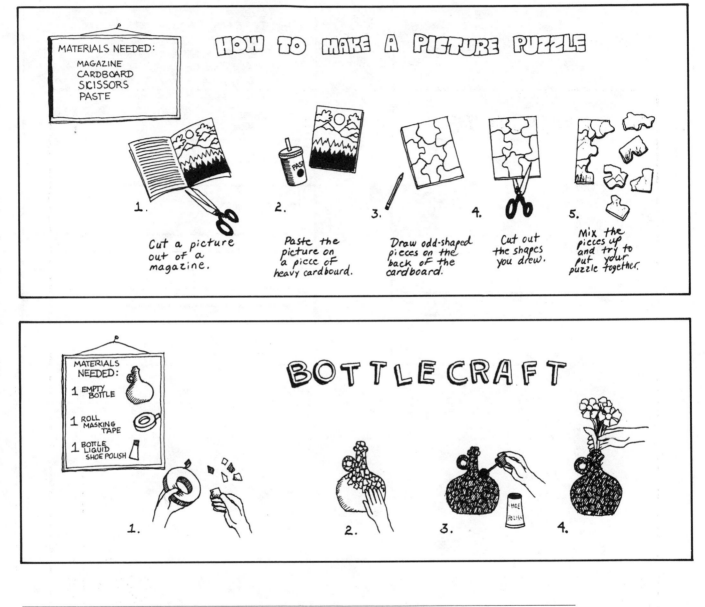

From *The Basics and Beyond* © 1981, Goodyear Publishing Co., Inc.

_____

_____

_____

_____

★ **PART II:** Below are two recipe cards. First read the sample recipe for Chicken Italiano. Then read the letter that follows, describing how to make Crunchy Apple Crisp. Underline all of the information in the letter that you would need to write a recipe for Crunchy Apple Crisp. Finally, write your recipe on the illustrated Crunchy Apple Crisp recipe card. Use the sample Chicken recipe card to help you organize your recipe.

FRONT

RECIPE FOR: CHICKEN ITALIANO

INGREDIENTS:
4 CHICKEN BREASTS
½ BOTTLE ITALIAN DRESSING
2 CUPS ITALIAN
       BREAD CRUMBS.

BACK

DIRECTIONS:
PREHEAT OVEN TO 400°.
POUR DRESSING INTO A BOWL.
DIP EACH CHICKEN PIECE IN THE
   DRESSING, THEN ROLL EACH
   PIECE IN THE BREADCRUMBS.
PLACE THE CHICKEN, SKIN SIDE
   UP, IN A 9" x 13" PAN.
BAKE FOR ONE HOUR.
SERVE OVER SPAGHETTI, IF DESIRED.
SERVES TWO.

FRONT

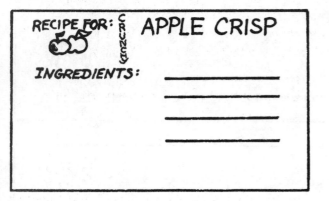

RECIPE FOR: CRUNCHY APPLE CRISP

INGREDIENTS: _____
_____
_____
_____

BACK

DIRECTIONS:
_____
_____
_____
_____
_____

SERVES _____.

Crunchy Apple Crisp

Dear friend,

    I thought that you might like these directions for making a great dessert called ***CRUNCHY APPLE CRISP***. It's simple to make, and it's a terrific way to end a meal!

    First, go to the store and buy all of the ingredients. Then, find a good place to work in your kitchen. You need to melt 2 tablespoons of butter and put the melted butter in one of those pans that is 9 inches across and 11 inches long (9 × 11). Then you have to slice 4 medium-sized apples (I forgot, you have to peel the apples first). Put the apple slices in the pan with the melted butter.

    Get out a large bowl and some measuring cups, and mix together ¾ cup flour, ¾ cup oatmeal, and ½ cup brown sugar. You can use a scoop or a spoon to fill up your measuring cups. Then mix in ½ cup of margarine. This mixture is a little hard to stir at first, but it will get more crumbly as you mix it. When it is crumbly, spread the mixture on top of the apples.

    Oh, by the way, you should have set the oven at 350º to preheat it before you started mixing the ingredients. Now put the pan in the oven and bake the dessert for 40 minutes. Don't forget to set a timer or look at a clock when you put the pan in the oven, so that you don't overbake the dessert.

    You should eat the apple crisp while it's still warm and crunchy! You might want to put some ice cream on top. I could eat the whole thing myself, but the apple crisp is supposed to be enough to serve 4 people. Enjoy it!

Crunchily,

A. Winesap

From *The Basics and Beyond* © 1981, Goodyear Publishing Co., Inc.

BONUS

★ **PART III:**   Create and write a recipe of your own, or write directions for a favorite arts and crafts project. See if a friend can successfully follow your recipe or craft directions. Write your directions on your own paper.

Where Do You Go from Here?

FIND IT! WRITE SOME DIRECTIONS TELLING HOW TO GET FROM ONE LOCATION TO ANOTHER

★ **PART I:** Two families, the Kampers and the Lodgers, are vacationing at Eagle Rock State Park. As the park ranger, you have been requested to give these families written directions to specific places within the park. Using the illustrated map of Eagle Rock State Park, fill in the necessary directions on the pictured memo forms.

EXAMPLE: from Jackson to the Fishing Area
Follow Route 42 across Swallow Bridge. Then drive along Park Drive to Chickasaw Lane. Stop where Chickasaw Lane and Arrowhead Drive meet. Walk on the marked foot trail to the fishing pier.

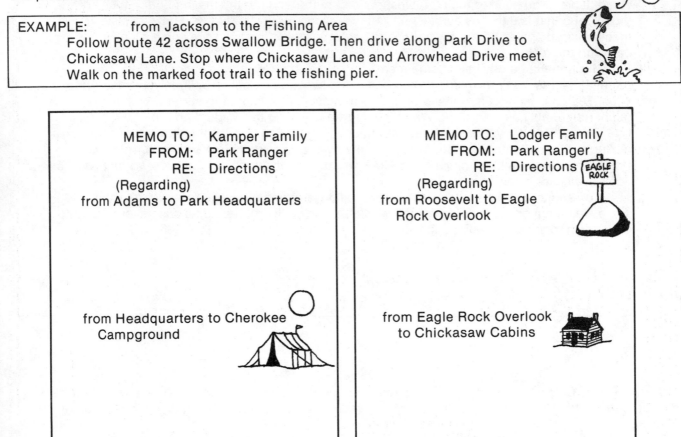

MEMO TO: Kamper Family
FROM: Park Ranger
RE: Directions
(Regarding)
from Adams to Park Headquarters

from Headquarters to Cherokee Campground

MEMO TO: Lodger Family
FROM: Park Ranger
RE: Directions
(Regarding)
from Roosevelt to Eagle Rock Overlook

from Eagle Rock Overlook to Chickasaw Cabins

From *The Basics and Beyond* © 1981, Goodyear Publishing Co., Inc.

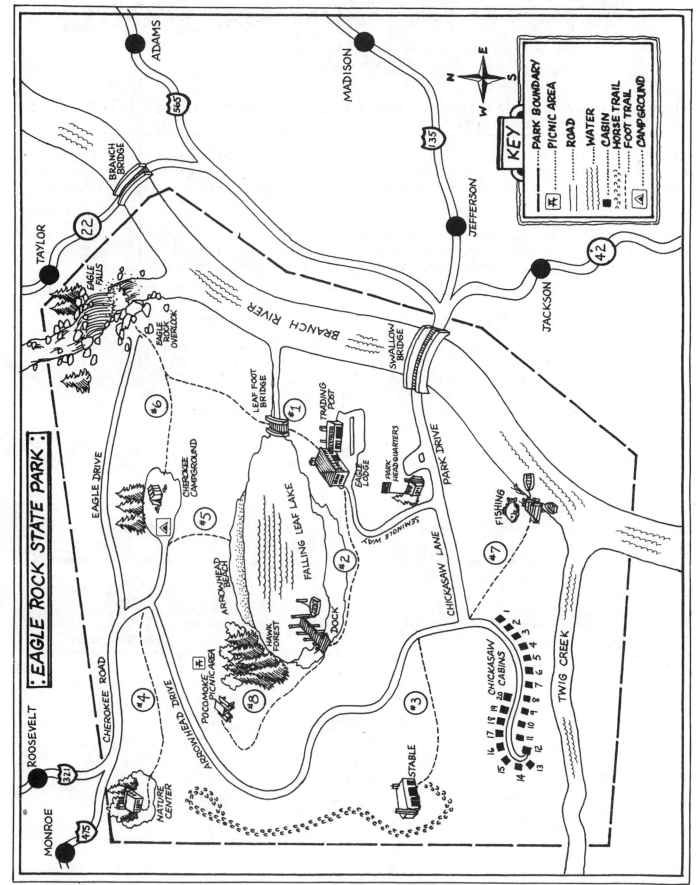

From *The Basics and Beyond* © 1981, Goodyear Publishing Co., Inc.

EAGLE ROCK STATE PARK

★ **PART II:** Choose two places within Eagle Rock State Park where you might decide to go. Write directions *to* each of those places *from* any of the towns on the map (Adams, Jefferson, Madison, Jackson, Taylor, Roosevelt, or Monroe).

from_____to_____

Directions:

from_____to_____

Directions:

BONUS

★ **PART III:** Choose the name of an area listed below. Draw a map of that area and write two sets of directions, each one telling how to get to a specific place shown on your map.

- Treasure Canyon
- Forbidden Forest
- Stellar Space Station

- Olympic Village
- Fantasy Island
- Terra Nova (a city of the future)

Organizing Outlines

An **OUTLINE** is a summary or means of organizing the main parts of a written work. An **OUTLINE** is divided into topics and subtopics.

ORGANIZE SOME SPEECHES USING OUTLINES

How to Write Outlines—Example

I. Purpose of Outlines
  A. Organize main ideas before completing a written work
    1. Reports
      a. School reports
      b. Business reports
    2. Speeches
  B. Summarize main ideas from a written work
II. Form of Outline
  A. Use *Roman Numerals* for main topic ideas
  B. Use *Capital Letters* for ideas about main topics
  C. Use *Numbers* for ideas about lettered topics
  D. Use *Lower Case Letters* for ideas about numbered topics
  E. Capitalize first letter of each topic
III. Topics in Outlines
  A. Number of Topics
    1. Must have at least two Roman Numerals
    2. *If* "A" is used, then "B" must be used
    3. *If* "1" is used, then "2" must be used
    4. *If* "a" is used, then "b" must be used
  B. Length of Topics
    1. Should tell only main ideas
    2. Should use phrases or brief sentences

"The Wise Kid Calculator"

Are you always complaining about your math grades? Then you need something that will help check your work, but does not give you the answers.

Buy this easy to operate pocket-sized calculator which runs on batteries or plugs into a socket. Make up your own problems and give the answers by pushing the correct buttons. This calculator is self-checking. If your answer is correct, a green light is lit and if your answer is wrong, a red light is lit. There are also 16,000 programmed math problems at four different levels of difficulty. The "Wise Kid" uses the four basic math operations.

This calculator comes in a variety of colors. You may buy it in blue, red, black, or green. Also, the sale price is only $7.99, reduced from the regular price of $8.99. Become a wise kid and buy the "Wise Kid Calculator" today!

Outline

I. Calculator's Advantages

   A. Checks your work

   B. Does not give you answers

II. Calculator's Features

   A. Easy to operate

      1. Pocket size

      2. Runs on Batteries

      3. _____

   B. Records math problems and answers when buttons are pushed

   C. Self-checking

      1. _____

      2. _____

   D. Has programmed math problems

      1. _____

      2. _____

   E. Uses the four math operations

III. Calculator's Description and Price

   A. _____

      1. Blue

      2. Red

      3. _____

      4. _____

   B. Price

      1. Regular $8.99

      2. _____

From *The Basics and Beyond* © 1981, Goodyear Publishing Co., Inc.

★ **PART II:** A speech was written to advertise the "Tuff Tennis Racket." Following the written speech, an outline was started to help the speaker tell about the racket, but not read the speech. Complete the outline by including all of the main ideas of the speech. (Note: Make sure that you follow all of the directions in the example.)

Tuff Tennis Racket

Are you tired of losing in tennis? You need a racket that will help you win. We have the winning racket with many great features. One feature our racket has is tough strings. This racket uses only Tuftex string which is as strong as gut, but costs less than gut. These tough strings give you the power to hit hard. Another feature which this racket has is its extra large head frame. This head is much larger than ordinary rackets and has a larger "sweet spot," which is the spot on the racket where you have the most ball control. In addition, the body frame feature comes in either graphite or wood so that every player can have it his or her way. Either frame is lightweight and easy to control. For an extra special feature, this racket has a grip that grips back. We use our exclusive Great Grip which helps to keep the racket from slipping out of your hand.

While you may find rackets that claim to have all of these features, you need some product facts. This racket is priced low and guaranteed for a full year. The price for this racket is only $19.99 which includes stringing. The guarantee is for a full money-back refund in 30 days (if you are not pleased with this racket) and a one-year guarantee on the entire frame. There is a 90-day guarantee on both the Tuftex string and on the Great Grip.

We can summarize this racket by saying—if you buy the Tuff Tennis Racket you won't need to pull strings; just use your head and get a great grip on things. Become a tough tennis player and get the Tuff Tennis Racket.

FRAME

SWEET SPOT

TUFTEX STRINGS

GREAT GRIP

Note: Complete this outline by organizing each paragraph under a separate roman numeral: I, II, III.

I. Features of Racket

II.

   A. Tough Strings

      1. Made of Tuftex

         a. Strong as gut

         b. Costs less than gut

      2. Power to hit hard

   B. Head Frame

      1. Extra large

      2. Larger "Sweet Spot"

   C. Body Frame

      1. Graphite

      2. Wood

      3. Lightweight

   D. Grip

      1. _____

      2. _____

★ PART III: From the following outline of "The Personalized Pet Place" you have been asked to write an advertisement which will be read on the radio. Complete the advertisement in the space provided.

THE PERSONALIZED PET PLACE

I. Pet Tags
   A. Identify pet
      1. Name
      2. Address
      3. Phone
   B. Give medical record
      1. Shots
      2. Medical problems

II. Pet Dishes
   A. Features
      1. Nonspill
      2. Dishwasher safe
      3. Many colors
         a. Red
         b. Blue
      4. Many types and sizes
         a. Double or single dishes
         b. Dog or cat dishes
   B. Personalized Printing
      1. Names
      2. Sayings

III. Pet Toys
IV. Pet Locations and Hours
   A. Five stores in area
   B. Open six days a week from 9:00 a.m. to 5:00 p.m.

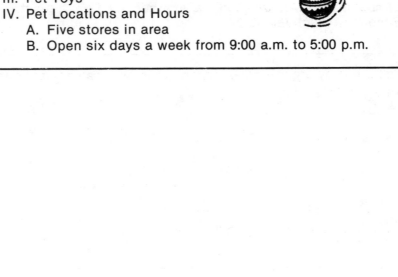

In Good Form

A **FORM** is a printed material used for reporting or recording specific information. Some types of **FORMS** are request forms, personal information forms, consumer forms, registrations, applications, opinion survey forms, order forms, and financial forms.

Example: Request Form

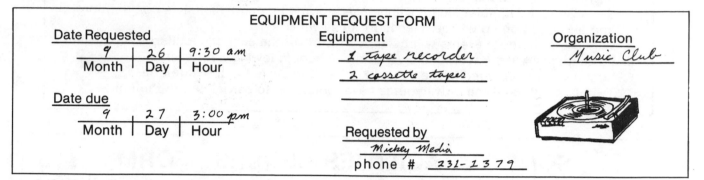

EQUIPMENT REQUEST FORM

Date Requested			Equipment	Organization
9	26	9:30 am	1 tape recorder	Music Club
Month	Day	Hour	2 cassette tapes	

Date due
9 | 27 | 3:00 pm
Month | Day | Hour

Requested by
Mickey Media
phone # 231-2379

REQUEST SOME SERVICES BY FILLING OUT FORMS

★ **PART I:**   You want to request a librarian to bring you the issues of materials (periodicals) listed below. Fill out the printed Periodical Request Form.

1. A June 15, 1975, issue of *Groove* Magazine.
2. A *Sport Stars* Magazine from 1968 (April 2).
3. A copy of the *New York Times* newspaper dated December 6, 1950.

PERIODICAL REQUEST FORM

Magazine _____

Newspaper _____

Microfilm _____

Name of person:

_____

Date of request _____

Name of periodical	Month	Day	Year
1.			
2.			
3.			
4.			
5.			
6.			

★ **PART II:** A club you belong to wants to use the facilities of an area high school for an all-day Sports Fair. Using the Sports Fair Information below, fill out the School Facilities Form that follows.

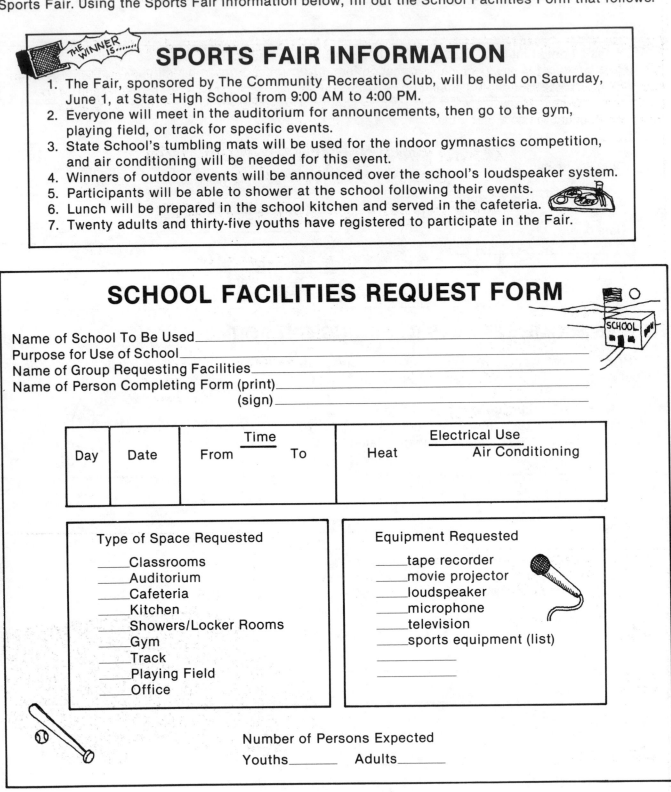

SPORTS FAIR INFORMATION

1. The Fair, sponsored by The Community Recreation Club, will be held on Saturday, June 1, at State High School from 9:00 AM to 4:00 PM.
2. Everyone will meet in the auditorium for announcements, then go to the gym, playing field, or track for specific events.
3. State School's tumbling mats will be used for the indoor gymnastics competition, and air conditioning will be needed for this event.
4. Winners of outdoor events will be announced over the school's loudspeaker system.
5. Participants will be able to shower at the school following their events.
6. Lunch will be prepared in the school kitchen and served in the cafeteria.
7. Twenty adults and thirty-five youths have registered to participate in the Fair.

SCHOOL FACILITIES REQUEST FORM

Name of School To Be Used_____

Purpose for Use of School_____

Name of Group Requesting Facilities_____

Name of Person Completing Form (print)_____

(sign) _____

Day	Date	Time From	To	Heat	Electrical Use — Air Conditioning

Type of Space Requested

_____Classrooms
_____Auditorium
_____Cafeteria
_____Kitchen
_____Showers/Locker Rooms
_____Gym
_____Track
_____Playing Field
_____Office

Equipment Requested

_____tape recorder
_____movie projector
_____loudspeaker
_____microphone
_____television
_____sports equipment (list)
_____
_____

Number of Persons Expected

Youths_____ Adults_____

From *The Basics and Beyond* © 1981, Goodyear Publishing Co., Inc.

For Your Information

COMPLETE SOME PERSONAL AND CONSUMER INFORMATION FORMS

★ **PART I:** You are moving from your present address to a new home in another state. The post office has given you some forms to fill out in a Change of Address Kit. Complete the forms below and let the publishers of *Groove* Magazine know where to forward your subscription. You will have to make up information telling the date you are moving and your new address.

When you move, this kit will help your mail move with you.

CHANGE OF ADDRESS KIT

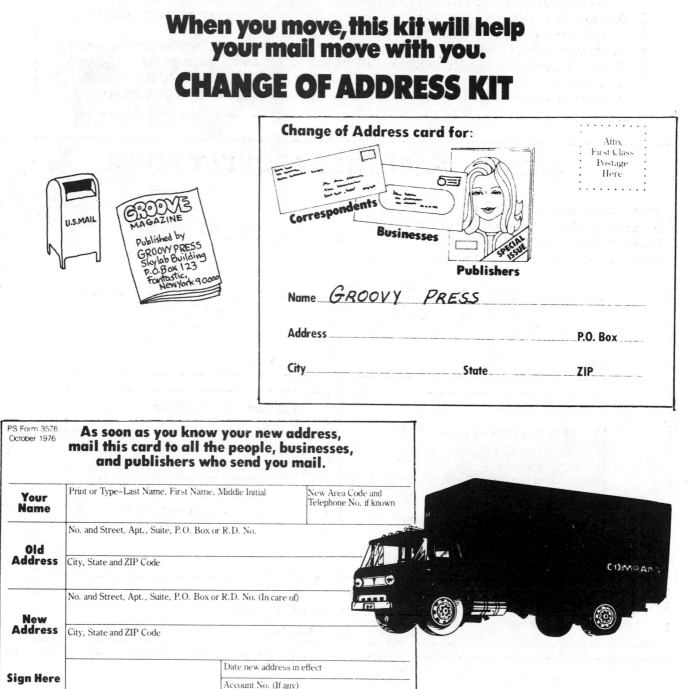

Change of Address card for:

Attix
First Class
Postage
Here

Correspondents

Businesses

Publishers

Name *GROOVY PRESS*

Address _____ P.O. Box _____

City _____ State _____ ZIP _____

PS Form 3576
October 1976

As soon as you know your new address, mail this card to all the people, businesses, and publishers who send you mail.

Your Name	Print or Type–Last Name, First Name, Middle Initial	New Area Code and Telephone No. if known
Old Address	No. and Street, Apt., Suite, P.O. Box or R.D. No.	
	City, State and ZIP Code	
New Address	No. and Street, Apt., Suite, P.O. Box or R.D. No. (In care of)	
	City, State and ZIP Code	
Sign Here	Date new address in effect	
	Account No. (If any)	

Receiver: Be sure to record the above new address in your address book at home or office.

★ **PART II:**   You have just purchased a Galaxy Nova space exploration game. Inside the game box you found the following Consumer Information Card from Goodenuff Products, the company that manufactures the game. Complete the form by using information on the pictured game box, and by making up any necessary additional information.

Goodenuff wants to do a better job for you.
Please fill out this CONSUMER INFORMATION CARD and return it to us. *Goodenuff* cares!

PRODUCT NAME_____ DATE PURCHASED_____

STORE WHERE PURCHASED_____ PRICE PAID_____

1. Where did you first learn about the game?

_____Saw on TV

_____Newspaper ad

_____In-store display

_____Friends have it

_____Brochure

_____In school

_____Magazine ad

_____Other_____

2. Who made the purchase?

_____Yourself   _____A relative   _____A friend

_____Age   _____Male   _____Female

3. Reason for buying this item:

_____Friends have it

_____Liked the package

_____Price

_____Gift

_____Educational game

_____Played with it in school

_____Other (please explain)

_____

_____

4. Do you like the item?   _____Yes   _____No

Why?_____

_____

5. Additional comments:_____

BONUS

★ **PART III:**   Create the name of a game or product. Design and make a Consumer Information Card that you might enclose with your game or product. On your card, include all of the information you would want to know from whomever purchased your product.

From *The Basics and Beyond* © 1981, Goodyear Publishing Co., Inc.

Apply Yourself

MAKE PLANS FOR THE SUMMER—APPLY TO AN OVERNIGHT CAMP

★ **PART I:** Fill out the Camp Wilderness application below, as if you were planning to attend camp the first two weeks in August.

CAMP WILDERNESS
SUMMER APPLICATION

In order to make your two-week stay with us more enjoyable, we would like to have the information requested below. Please complete all items on this form.

I. PERSONAL INFORMATION

Name_____ Date _____

Address _____

Home Phone_____

Date of Birth_____ Height_____ Weight_____

Camp Session you plan to attend (check one)

July 1–15_____

July 16–31_____

August 1–15_____

II. HEALTH

1. Do you have any allergies? No_____ Yes_____
   If yes, please list things you are allergic to:

   _____

2. Do you have any health problems that might interfere with outdoor activities such as swimming, hiking, or horseback riding? No_____ Yes_____

   If yes, please describe problems: _____

   _____

3. Who can be contacted in case of emergency?

   Name_____ Phone _____

III. CAMP EXPERIENCE

1. Have you ever attended camp before?

   No   Yes   How Many Years?

   Day Camp

   Overnight Camp

2. If you attended overnight camp before, describe what you liked best about that camp

   experience. _____

   _____

From *The Basics and Beyond* © 1981, Goodyear Publishing Co., Inc.

IV. Interests

1. From the list below, find and check three activities in which you would like to participate most. List your three choices in order of preference in the spaces provided.

_____ tennis

_____ baseball

_____ soccer

_____ archery

_____ basketball

_____ swimming

_____ sailing

_____ canoeing

_____ fishing

_____ hiking

_____ backpacking

_____ animal study

_____ horseback riding

_____ dramatics

_____ group singing

_____ square dancing

_____ arts and crafts

1st choice

_____

2nd choice

_____

3rd choice

_____

2. Name any of your other special interests or hobbies.

_____

V. SKILLS

Check the column that you feel best describes your skill level in each area listed below.

	No Previous Experience	Beginning Level	Intermediate Level	Advanced Level
Swimming	_____	_____	_____	_____
Diving	_____	_____	_____	_____
Canoeing	_____	_____	_____	_____
Sailing	_____	_____	_____	_____
Horseback Riding	_____	_____	_____	_____
Tennis	_____	_____	_____	_____

From *The Basics and Beyond* © 1981, Goodyear Publishing Co., Inc.

VI. NATURE STUDY

1. Check the two topics that you would most like to study at camp.

_____identifying plants and trees

_____pond life

_____identifying animal tracks

_____wild plants you can eat

_____birds

_____rocks and minerals

_____snakes and other reptiles

_____forest mammals

_____insects

_____weather

_____other (list topic)

_____

2. Write one question about plant or animal life that you would like to find the answer to while at camp.

_____

_____

VII. GENERAL

In one or two sentences, explain why you want to attend Camp Wilderness, and what you hope to gain from your camp experience.

_____

_____

THANK YOU! We look forward to seeing you at Camp Wilderness this summer!

BONUS

★ **PART II:** Make up your own application form for a special program. Choose one of the topics listed below, or create a topic of your own.

- swim team
- soccer camp
- theater workshop
- summer school
- membership in a club
- scout group

Opinion Please

An **OPINION POLL** is a series of statements or questions about which people are asked to state or write their personal views.

PARTICIPATE IN AN OPINION POLL ABOUT TELEVISION VIEWING

★ **PART I:** Complete the following opinion poll.

TELEVISION RESEARCH, INC. Viewer Opinion Poll

Name_____ Age_____

A. Answer the following questions by checking the correct response.

1. How many TV sets do you have in your home?

   0_____ 1_____ 2_____ more than 2_____

2. Where are your TV sets located?

   living room_____ kitchen_____ den_____ family room_____

   bedroom_____ basement_____ other_____

3. About how many hours per day do you watch TV on weekdays (Monday–Friday)?

   0-2_____ 2-4_____ 4-6_____ 6-8_____ more than 8_____

4. About how many hours per day do you watch TV on weekends (Saturday and Sunday)?

   0-2_____ 2-4_____ 4-6_____ 6-8_____ more than 8_____

B. On a scale of 1 to 5, circle the number that most nearly gives your opinion about the statements below.

	STRONGLY AGREE 1	AGREE 2	NO OPINION 3	DISAGREE 4	STRONGLY DISAGREE 5
1. There is too much violence on TV.	1	2	3	4	5
2. Watching violence on TV causes people to act violently.	1	2	3	4	5
3. TV presents a realistic view of our society.	1	2	3	4	5
4. Parents should limit the time their children watch TV.	1	2	3	4	5
5. The government should decide what is shown on TV.	1	2	3	4	5
6. Watching a story on TV is more enjoyable than reading the same story in a book.	1	2	3	4	5
7. Watching a sports event on TV is more enjoyable than attending the event.	1	2	3	4	5

C. Complete each sentence below with a word or brief statement.

1. There are too many _____ on television.

2. There are not enough _____ on television.

3. I enjoy TV shows that _____

_____.

4. I dislike TV shows that _____

_____.

5. I enjoy TV commercials that _____

_____.

6. I dislike TV commercials that _____

_____.

7. If I were to create a new television show, it would be called _____ and it

would be about _____.

D. Write any additional comments you wish to make about TV viewing.

BONUS

★ **PART II:** Make up your own opinion poll about a topic of your choice. (Suggested topics: Movies, Team sports, Homework, Chores)

From *The Basics and Beyond* © 1981, Goodyear Publishing Co., Inc.

Send-Away

An **ORDER FORM** provides a format for summarizing information necessary for a consumer to describe and order specific products from a company.

ORDER YOUR PERSONALIZED NOTE PADS AND PENS FROM A MAIL-ORDER COMPANY

★ Choose to order one or more of each of the following: the memo pads, the Super Pens, and the jumbo memo pads. Then fill in all of the appropriate forms below. (Note: Superflow Stationery is not a real company. Please do not actually mail the order forms.)

Pens and Pads by Superflow

PERSONALIZED "MEMO PADS"   ITEM #43

2 PADS only $1.00
(100 SHEETS PER PAD)

JUST LIKE THE ONES EXECUTIVES USE! EACH 4"x 5" SHEET IS CLEARLY PRINTED WITH "FROM THE DESK OF" FOLLOWED BY YOUR NAME. PERFECT FOR HOME OR SCHOOL. WHITE PAPER ONLY.

SEND ME _____ MEMO PAD SET(S) AS DESCRIBED AT $1.00 PER SET, PLUS .25¢ FOR POSTAGE & HANDLING.

Same name must appear on both pads in each set.

Personalize as follows: (Please Print)

Set #1_____

Set #2_____

Set #3_____

"SUPER PENS"   ITEM #45

5 FOR $1.00
PERSONALIZED WITH YOUR NAME IN BRIGHT GOLD

(AVAILABLE COLORS : BLUE, RED, GREEN, OR BLACK)

SHOP IN THE COMFORT OF YOUR HOME AND GET FIVE HIGH QUALITY RETRACTABLE BALLPOINT PENS PERSONALIZED WITH YOUR NAME IN GOLD. EACH PEN WRITES WITH BLUE INK. A GREAT GIFT.

SEND ME _____ SET(S) OF FIVE SUPER PERSONALIZED PENS (AS DESCRIBED) AT $1.00 PER SET, PLUS .25¢ FOR POSTAGE & HANDLING.

Same name must appear on all 5 pens in each set. Name limited to 20 characters and spaces.

Personalize as follows: (Please Print)

Set #1_____

Set #2_____

PERSONALIZED "JUMBO MEMO PAD"   ITEM #47

ONLY $1.00
(100 SHEETS PER PAD)

NEW JUMBO 5"x8" MEMO PAD WITH YOUR NAME PRINTED ON EVERY SHEET. PERFECT FOR HOME OR SCHOOL. WHITE PAPER ONLY.

SEND ME _____ JUMBO PERSONALIZED MEMO PAD(S) (AS DESCRIBED) AT $1.00 PER PAD, PLUS .25¢ FOR POSTAGE AND HANDLING.

Personalize as follows: (Please Print)

Pad 1._____

Pad 2._____

From *The Basics and Beyond* © 1981, Goodyear Publishing Co., Inc.

ORDER FORM

PLESE NOTE: • Send cash, check, or money order
- • Use plain paper for additional orders
- • Allow 3 to 4 weeks for delivery
- • Add 25¢ postage and handling charge only once to each total order

SUPERFLOW Stationery Company
195 Line Drive
Writer's Cramp, New York 00034

Shipping Label (please print)

Name _____

Address _____
(street)   (city)   (state)   (ZIP code)

QUANTITY	ITEM NUMBER	SIZE OR COLOR	DESCRIPTION OR TITLE	PRICE	AMOUNT
			Postage and Handling	25	25
			TOTAL AMOUNT OF ORDER ►		

All prices include tax:

JUMBO MEMO PAD !

APPENDIX A
Practical Proofreading

PROOFREADING is rereading material and making any necessary corrections.

AFTER WRITING ANY ACTIVITY, PROOFREAD YOUR OWN WORK

GUIDELINES FOR PROOFREADING (what to look for)

- Do all sentences express a complete thought?
- Do all sentences contain a subject and predicate?
- Do all sentences begin with capital letters?
- Do all sentences end with either a period, question mark, or exclamation point?
- Are capital letters used appropriately?
- Are punctuation marks—commas, period, question marks, exclamation points, colons, semicolons, quotation marks, apostrophes, parentheses, dashes, hyphens, and ellipses—used appropriately?
- Are all words spelled correctly? (If unsure, check a dictionary.)
- Is all necessary information included in your written paragraph, correspondence, form, schedule, message, outline, or other material?

TECHNIQUES FOR PROOFREADING (how to do it)

- Proofread your material by slowly reading each sentence aloud to yourself.
- Be aware that some changes in writing may make other changes necessary.
- Make the appropriate corrections or changes and proofread again.
- After making all corrections or changes rewrite the material neatly and proofread a final time.
- Optional: Have someone else proofread the material for any errors you may have overlooked.

From *The Basics and Beyond* © 1981, Goodyear Publishing Co., Inc.

APPENDIX B
Additional Practical
Writing Ideas and Resources

IDEAS FOR DEVELOPING PRACTICAL WRITING ACTIVITIES

Unlimited practical writing activities may be suggested by and developed around the wide variety of materials and events present in our daily lives. Listed below are possible student activities related to utilizing just one source—the newspaper.

NEWSPAPER ACTIVITIES

- Schedules. Prepare a personal activity schedule for one day, based on newspaper listings of area entertainment, civic, or sports events.
- Calendars. Plan a weekly calendar of things to do based on descriptions of entertainment and community events noted in the newspaper.
- Lists. List people in the news you'd like to meet; list newspaper sale items you'd like to buy; list movies you'd like to see.
- Logs and Journals. Write log or journal entries based on events described in news or feature stories.
- Resumés. Prepare a resumé appropriate for use in applying for a job advertised in the want ads or for a job of a person discussed in a news story.
- Telephone Messages. Select a classified ad and imagine that you are the person advertising that item. Write a phone message you might take after speaking to someone who has responded to your ad.
- Memos. Write a memo to the newspaper carrier reminding him or her not to deliver the paper while you're away on vacation; write a memo to a friend requesting that he or she read a particular article of interest.
- Notices. Write a notice for the classified advertising section; write an ad for a listed TV show or movie; write a lost and found notice.
- Announcements and Posters. Select an event mentioned in the newspaper and create an announcement or poster for that event.
- Invitations. Write an invitation to a person in the news asking him or her to come to speak to a class or club of which you are a member.
- Notes. Write a congratulations note to someone you read about in the paper who has won an election, award, or sports event.
- Greeting Cards. Create and send a get well card to someone mentioned in the newspaper who is sick or injured.
- Telegrams. Write and send a public opinion message to a national or local public official about an issue discussed in the newspaper.
- Postcards. Create and send a picture postcard as if you were vacationing in a place described in the travel section of the newspaper.
- Informal Letters. Write a letter to one of the advice columns that appear in your local paper; write a letter to a comic strip character.
- Formal Letters. Write a letter of request asking for specific information about a topic featured in the newspaper (recipe exchange, pet care advice, travel notices, etc.); write a letter to the editor about a topic of interest to you; write an opinion column about the same television show or movie reviewed by the newspaper drama critic.
- Directions. Rewrite newspaper recipes; write directions to accompany newspaper photographs of machines or products; write directions telling how to order home delivery of the newspaper or how to place a classified ad in the paper; write directions telling someone how to get to the place where an event mentioned in the paper is being held.
- Outlining. Outline news articles or stories told in comic strips.
- Other. Write songs or jingles, business cards, bumper stickers, or message buttons to convince others to order a particular newspaper.

From *The Basics and Beyond* © 1981, Goodyear Publishing Co., Inc.

RESOURCES FOR DEVELOPING PRACTICAL WRITING ACTIVITIES

The following resources are appropriate for use in obtaining free and inexpensive materials and in developing ideas for practical writing programs. They can be used to provide ideas for practical writing programs. They can be used to provide motivation for students to write lists, schedules, logs, journals, memos, notices, advertisements, messages, letters, directions, and forms.

BOOKS

Abruscato, Joe, and Jack Hassard. *The Earthpeople Activity Book: People, Places, Pleasures, and Other Delights.* Santa Monica, Calif.: Goodyear, 1978. (suitable for motivating a variety of categorizing, listing, and journaling activities)

Aubrey, Ruth, H. *Selected Free Materials for Classroom Teachers.* Belmont, Calif.: Fearon Press, 1975. (lists thousands of free items that can be ordered through the mail; suitable for a variety of correspondence activities)

Bogojavlensky, Ann, and Donna Grossman, et. al. *The Great Learning Book.* Reading, Mass.: Addison-Wesley, 1977. (presents a variety of learning activities based on real-world occupations and experiences; also lists sources for obtaining materials)

Cardozo, Peter, *The Whole Kids' Catalog.* New York: Bantam Books, 1975. (includes listing of sources of free and inexpensive materials, science and art activities, information on hobbies and special interests of students; suitable for stimulating interest in listing, journaling, writing correspondence, writing directions)

Holland, Margaret, and Alison Strickland. *The Listing Book,* School Book Fairs, Inc., New York, 1978. (presents high-interest topics and activity sheets for student use in preparing a variety of organizational lists; also suitable for activities related to journaling)

Masden, Sheila, and Bette Gould. *The Teachers' Book of Lists.* Santa Monica, Calif.: Goodyear, 1979. (suitable for motivating ideas for writing based on lists ranging from Actors/Actresses to Olympic Events to Zany People)

Wurman, Richard Saul. *Yellow Pages of Learning Resources.* Cambridge, Mass.: MIT Press, 1972. (presents ideas for students on how to gain information from their own environment; utilizes a Yellow Pages telephone directory format; suitable for encouraging formal and informal types of correspondence)

From *The Basics and Beyond* © 1981, Goodyear Publishing Co., Inc.

PEOPLE, PLACES, ORGANIZATIONS

merchants

advertisers

researchers

pollsters

public officials

game designers and manufacturers

artists

drama critics

newspaper, magazine editors

coaches and team managers

Western Union

local, state, and federal government agencies

colleges, universities

recreation departments

businesses

Pen Pal organizations

embassies

travel agencies

libraries

hospitals

**OTHER
(add your
own ideas)**

_____

_____

_____

_____

_____

_____

_____

MATERIALS

catalogs

advertisements

newspapers

magazines

political literature

travel, tourist literature

song sheets

greeting cards

bumper stickers

message buttons

announcements

phone books

posters

recipes

arts and crafts books

maps

consumer pamphlets

business, professional cards

forms

applications

product information brochures

schedules

calendars

charts

fliers

**OTHER
(add your
own ideas)**

_____

_____

_____

_____

_____

_____

_____

From *The Basics and Beyond* © 1981, Goodyear Publishing Co., Inc.

Answer Keys

From *The Basics and Beyond* © 1981, Goodyear Publishing Co., Inc.

UNIT 1   TODAY: Develop Your Skills

SECTION ONE
Traveling Through the World of Words

VACATION WITH NOUNS
PART I—Common Nouns

1–islands, valleys, beaches; 2–ranches, island;
3–plantations, fields; 4–beaches, forest, village;
5–place, life, beaches; 6–island, farms, volcano

Proper Nouns

1–Kauai; 2–Molokai; 3–Lanai; 4–Maui; 5–Oahu,
Honolulu; 6–Hawaii, Kilauea

PART II—Nouns

Hawaiian Islands, stretch, ocean, reefs, coral, crests,
mountains, islands, things, people, scientists,
laboratory, plants, animals, state, Union, home

PRONOUN HOLIDAY
PART I

1–you; 2–they; 3–you; 4–we; 5–you; 6–its; 7–we;
8–you; 9–I; 10–this; 11–his; 12–her; 13–your;
14–your; 15–our; 16–we; 17–you; 18–your; 19–us

PART II

1–it; 2–their; 3–its; 4–they; 5–her; 6–them

HIGHLIGHTING HAWAII WITH VERBS
PART I

☑

PART II

come, fly, enjoy, is, lives, are, approach, will see,
stands, etched, is, shop, has been, tour, hear,
happened, rent, drive, visit, taste, is, search, are
hidden, see, will be

COOK WITH GRAMMAR
PART I—Nouns

butter, skillet, chicken, pepper, pineapple, syrup,
water, cups, mixture, vinegar, cornstarch, sugar,
mustard, sauce, minutes, rice

Verbs

melt, stir, drain, measure, add, blend, pour, cook, stir,
cover, simmer, serve

PART II

1–e; 2–a; 3–f; 4–c; 5–d; 6–b

PART III

☑

ALOHA ADVENTURES
WITH ADJECTIVES AND ADVERBS
PART I

1–f; 2–l; 3–d; 4–b; 5–a; 6–i; 7–j; 8–c,e,h; 9–g; 10–k

PART II

1–e; 2–i; 3–h; 4–c; 5–f; 6–d; 7–j; 8–l, 9–b; 10–k; 11–a; 12–g

SOUVENIR SHOPPING

☑

ADVERTISING
WITH VERBS AND ADVERBS
PART I

☑

PART II

1–early; 2–more, little, almost, everything;
3–everywhere; 4–late; 5–most, much; 6–anywhere

PART III

☑

WORD CHAINS
PART I

☑

PART II

☑

PART III

☑

DIVE FOR PREPOSITIONS
PART I—Prepositions

1–onto; 2–over; 3–in; 4–on, of; 5–(none); 6–toward;
7–at; 8–up, in, at; 9–under; 10–underneath

PART II

1–onto your feet; 2–over your eyes and nose; 3–in
your mouth; 4–on the surface, of the water; 5–(none);
6–toward the bottom; 7–at the waist; 8–up in the air,
at the bottom; 9–under the water; 10–underneath the
surface

PART III

☑

PREPOSITION PUZZLE
PART I

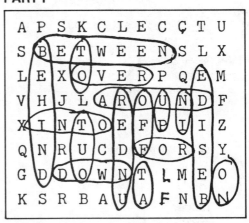

PART II

☑

TOUR WITH CONJUNCTIONS

1–while; 2–and; 3–either; 4–or; 5–but; 6–if; 7–unless;
8–for; 9–neither; 10–nor

SURF WITH INTERJECTIONS
PART I

☑

PART II

☑

NO NONSENSE
PART I
☞
PART II
☞

HAWAIIAN ISLAND HOP
Could you play the game successfully?

RESTAURANT REVIEW SYNONYMS
PART I
☞
PART II
1–h; 2–o; 3–n; 4–k; 5–j; 6–a; 7–i; 8–b; 9–l; 10–g;
11–m; 12–c; 13–d; 14–f; 15–e

ANTONYM MESSAGES
PART I
☞
PART II
☞

HOMOPHONE HAPPENINGS
PART I
1–morning; 2–due; 3–rain; 4–eight; 5–so; 6–see;
7–there; 8–weather; 9–site; 10–fourth; 11–hear;
12–red; 13–sun; 14–sea; 15–seen; 16–we; 17–one;
18–you
PART II
☞

COMPOUND CROSSWORDS
Down   1–foothill; 3–land; 4–day; 5–underground;
       6–surf; 7–suntan; 9–waterfall; 13–horse;
       15–over
Across 2–worldwide; 7–sunset; 8–your; 10–air;
        11–torchlight; 12–trip; 14–note; 16–sail;
        17–door; 18–glasses

COMPOUND CREATIONS
PART I
1–sailboat; 2–lighthouse; 3–notebook; 4–swordfish;
5–forehead; 6–sunglasses; 7–rainbow
PART II
☞
PART III
☞

TAKE OFF WITH AFFIXES
PART I

	PREFIX	ROOT	SUFFIX
1.	ultra	modern	
2.	super	sonic	
3.		effort	less, ly
4.		steward	ess
5.		warm	ly
6.		complete	ly
7.		comfort	able
8.	de	part	ure
9.		familiar	ize
10.		instruct	ions
11.	multi	level	
12.	anti	static	
13.		music	al
14.	en	joy	ment
15.	self	adjusting	
16.	un	loading	
17.		happy	ness
18.	fore	most	
19.	non	stop	
20.		care	free
21.		excite	ment
22.	dis	satisfied	
23.	re	fund	
24.	pre	paid	

PART II
☞

SECTION TWO
Communicating Through the World of Sentences

FOOTBALL FACTS
PART I

	Subjects	Predicates
1.	Redskins	Hold (or Holdoff)
2.	Rams	Blank
3.	Jets	Edge
4.	Campbell	Leads
5.	Dolphins	Rip
6.	Bears	Sink
7.	Bengals	Beat
8.	Cardinals	Beaten
9.	Whitehurst	Bombs
10.	Vikings	Host

PART II
☞
PART III
☞

TENNIS TOPICS
PART I
1. Liz Severt, America's tennis queen
2. The 2-handed backhand player, Severt
3. The 2 women
4. Their scores
5. Stacy Tossin, who has been referred to in the past as Stacy in Wonderland
6. She
7. The tennis challenger of the future, Tossin
8. Soon Severt
PART II
1. can keep on your toes, run faster, and stay out in front with Supertoes tennis shoes.
2. help you keep your balance and give you a better chance to win the game.
3. are made of durable materials.
4. will all enjoy staying in shape and exercising with Supertoes tennis shoes.

PART III
☑
CONFUSED NEWS
☑
VIDEO PHRASES
☑
PHRASE-A-PRODUCT
PART I
Kitten's Meow—1–to adult cats; 2–including extra vitamins; 3–strong teeth; 4–from any grocery store near you.
PART II
☑
WINNERS/LOSERS
☑
GET IN THE GROOVE
☑
COMEDY CORNER
PART I
1–d, 2–h, 3–c, 4–i, 5–a, 6–e, 7–g, 8–j, 9–f, 10–b
PART II
☑
BUTTON MESSAGES
PART I
1. Carpenters shouldn't bite their nails.
2. All teachers have class.
3. Skunks have uncommon scents.
4. A woman's place is in the House and in the Senate.
5. Soccer players get a kick out of life.
6. Quarterbacks are on the ball.
7. Prunes are really the pits.
8. Golfers are up to par.
9. Astronauts are out of this world.
10. Carter worked for peanuts.
PART II
☑
COMPOUND CAPTIONS
☑
COMPLEX COPY
☑
1–c, 2–f, 3–a, 4–e, 5–d, 6–b
COMPLEX COP-OUTS
☑
TV TALK: STATE YOUR SENTENCE
PART I
1–S, 2–Q, 3–S, 4–C, 5–E, 6–Q
PART II
☑
PART III
☑

CORRECT CAPITALS
PART I
Police, Uncover, Masked, Bandit, Speedy, Wire, Service, on, Friday, January, Nine, Corners, Medical, Building, Funfax, Virginia, Doctor, Ivan, Ben, Taken's, On, Saturday, Dr., Taken, However, Sunday, Dr., Taken's, When, Dr., Ivan, B., Taken, These, Only, I, That, Sunday, Funfax, Police, Department, No, However, Monday, Finally, At, Dr., Taken, Funfax, Police, Department, A, Our, So.
PART II
A) On, On, However, Sunday, When, Only, I, That, No, However, Finally, At, A, Our, So;
B) Speedy, Wire, Service, Nine, Corners, Medical, Building, Funfax, Virginia, Ivan, Ben, Taken's, Dr., Taken, Dr., Taken's, Dr., Ivan, B., Taken, Funfax, Police, Department, Dr., Taken, Funfax, Police, Department;
C) Friday, January, Saturday, Sunday, Sunday, Monday;
D) Police, Uncover, Masked, Bandit;
E) These.
CAPITALIZE ON THIS
PART I
A) 1–The, 2–Teddy, 3–Sarah, 4–Newburg, 5–Zoo, 6–In, 7–The, 8–Mr., 9–Joseph, 10–R., 11–Bars, 12–Dallas, 13–Texas;
B) 1–Suzanne, 2–Sally, 3–Tuesday, 4–April, 5–Since, 6–Mr., 7–Joseph, 8–R., 9–Bars, 10–These, 11–I
PART II
☑
SPEAKING OF SPORTS
☑
COMMA CINEMA
See the all new space adventure, "Return to Galaxy Nova," coming soon to neighborhood theaters. Thrill at the incredible special effects, as starships clash, rockets explode, and planets collide! Because you've been waiting so long for this film, the producers have spared no expense in bringing you a dramatic, fast-paced, amusing, and heartwarming story. The Gazette's movie critic, C. A. Film, has commented, "This is the space adventure of all times!"

"Return to Galaxy Nova" will premiere in Boston, Massachusetts, on Friday, January 1. It will open at a theater near you on Saturday, January 15, and it is sure to bring you hours of pleasure. If you enjoy chills and thrills, don't miss it!
COMMA CONFUSION
1–you went with Alex Charles, Jill Phillips, and Greg to the movies; 2–Newburg School's basketball team will play Jackson, which tied Jefferson, and Adams; 3–I'm coming to the party with Julie, Harris; 4–Don't play the piano, or drum with your fingers.

RIDDLED QUOTES
PART I
(Sentences may also be written in different order. See answer one as an example.)

1. ''You make me flip my lid,'' said the can to the can opener. The can opener said to the can, ''You make me flip my lid.''
2. ''You can count on me,'' said the adding machine to the cashier.
3. ''One more crack and I'll plaster you!'' said the painter to the wall.
4. ''Take me to your weeder,'' one dandelion said to the other.
5. ''Don't move, I've got you covered,'' said the rug to the floor.
6. George Washington said to his men before they crossed the Delaware River, ''Get in the boat.''
7. ''Whoa!'' Paul Revere said at the end of his famous ride.
8. One duck said to the other duck, ''You quack me up.''
9. ''Let's go out tonight,'' said one light to the other light.
10. ''Let's meet at the corner,'' said one wall to the other wall.

PART II
☛

PUNCTUATION PUNS
PART I
1. ''The water is fine,'' called Tom swimmingly.
2. ''I love chocolate,'' Tom commented sweetly.
3. Tom asked heartily, ''Is it Valentine's Day?''
4. Tom replied off-handedly, ''I'll never feed a lion again.''
5. ''I'm a prince,'' Tom remarked charmingly.
6. ''The rain ruined our picnic,'' Tom grumbled stormily.

PART II
☛

WILDLIFE TRIVIA
PART I
1–e, 2–d, 3–g, 4–b, 5–f, 6–c, 7–a, 8–h

PART II
1. (none live near the North Pole)
2. (with the oldest recorded age of a tortoise being 16)
3. (which lives along the gulf coast of Texas)
4. (all found in Australia)
5. (the cat on television commercials for 9-Lives Cat Food)

PUNCTUATION PRESS
☛

MARK MY WORDS
☛

From *The Basics and Beyond* © 1981, Goodyear Publishing Co., Inc.

UNIT 2 TOMORROW: APPLY YOUR SKILLS

SECTION ONE
The Real World: Recording Personal Information

IT'S IN THE SCHEDULE
10:00, parade; 10:30, jugglers; 2:00, firefighters; 11:00 or 2:30, band concert; other events and times are flexible

CALENDAR COUNTDOWN
Monday, 1:00 student council meeting; Tuesday, 4:30 music lesson; Wednesday, 5:00 dentist appointment; Thursday, 4:00 pick up dog; Friday (morning), science report due, 7:00 haircut; Saturday, return library books, 1:00 bowling, 2:00 movie; Sunday, 6:00 dinner at Uncle Alan's

MAKE A LIST
☛

LOOKING AT LOGS
PART I

THURSDAY
9:00 AM	left headquarters
10:00-12:00	arrived and unpacked
12:00-12:15	flag-raising
12:15-1:00	lunch
1:00-2:00	orientation hike
2:00-4:30	forestry hike
4:30-5:15	free time (volleyball)
5:15-5:30	KP duty
5:30-6:30	supper
6:30-6:45	flag-lowering
6:45-8:00	free time (ping pong)
8:00-9:30	ecology movie
9:30 PM	lights out

FRIDAY
7:00-8:00 AM	wake up, clean bunks
8:00-8:15	flag-raising
8:15-9:00	breakfast
9:00-12:00	ecology hike
12:00-1:00	lunch
1:00-2:00	free time
2:00-4:00	farm visit
4:00-4:15	flag-lowering
4:15-5:15	return to Outobon Society

PART II
☞
PART III
☞
JOURNAL JOURNEY
☞
RESUMÉ REVIEW
☞

SECTION TWO
The Real World:
Responding to the Demands of Society

WHILE YOU WERE OUT
PART I
Message #1: From–*Alex Bell*; For–*parents*;
Date & Time–*March 3rd, 5:30 p.m.*;
Message–☞ ; Message Taken
By–*Sid*
Message #2: From–*Betty Barker*; For–*Derek*; Date
& Time–*March 5th, 3:00 p.m.*;
Message–☞ ; Message Taken
By–*Alison*

PART II
☞
MEMO MADNESS
☞

☞
RESUMÉ REVIEW
☞
POST A NOTICE
PART I
Reggie Jackson-Pete Rose; Rolling Pebble can-Kool
or Mudweiser can; stamp from Morocco-stamped
envelope from Kenya; Superman comic-Spiderman
comic
PART II
☞
PART III
☞
THE MAIN EVENTS
☞
YOU'RE INVITED
☞
NOTE THIS
☞
GREETINGS
☞
TELEGRAM TOPICS
☞
POSTCARD PRACTICE
☞
PERSONALLY SPEAKING
☞
MINDING YOUR OWN BUSINESS
☞

CONSUMER COMPLAINT
☞
CRITIC'S CHOICE
☞
REVIEWING REQUESTS
☞
DIRECT DIRECTIONS
☞
EASY EXPLANATIONS
☞
CRAFT AND COOKING CORNER
☞
WHERE DO YOU GO FROM HERE?
☞
ORGANIZING OUTLINES
PART I
II A. 3   Plugs into socket
II C. 1   Green light for right answer
II C. 2   Red light for wrong answer
II D. 1   Has 16,000 problems
II D. 2   Has four levels of difficulty
III A.   Many colors
III A. 3   Black
III A. 4   Green
III B. 2   Sale $7.99
PART II
☞
PART III
☞
IN GOOD FORM
PART I
1. *Groove Magazine,* June 15, 1975
2. *Sport Stars Magazine,* April 2, 1968
3. *New York Times Newspaper,* December 6, 1950
PART II
Name of School – State High School
Purpose – Sports Fair
Group – Community Recreation Club
Day – Saturday   Date – June 1   Time – 9:00-4:00
Electrical Use – air conditioning
Space – auditorium, cafeteria, kitchen, showers, gym,
                track, field, office (possibly)
Youth-35, Adult-20   Equipment – loudspeaker, sport
                                                    (mats)

FOR YOUR INFORMATION
PART I
☞
PART II
product – Galaxy Nova Game; store – Toytown; price
$3.95; rest of form ☞
PART III
☞
APPLY YOURSELF
☞
OPINION PLEASE
☞
SEND-AWAY
☞

From *The Basics and Beyond* © 1981, Goodyear Publishing Co., Inc.